CLASSICAL WOMEN POETS

CLASSICAL WOMEN POETS

TRANSLATED &
INTRODUCED BY

JOSEPHINE
BALMER

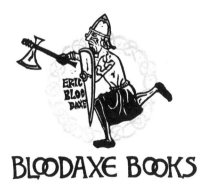

BLOODAXE BOOKS

ISBN: 1 85224 342 2

First published 1996 by
Bloodaxe Books Ltd,
P.O. Box 1SN,
Newcastle upon Tyne NE99 1SN.

Bloodaxe Books Ltd acknowledges
the financial assistance of Northern Arts.

Cover printing by J. Thomson Colour Printers Ltd, Glasgow.

Printed in Great Britain by
Cromwell Press Ltd, Broughton Gifford, Melksham, Wiltshire.

for

P.D.

s.q.n.

ACKNOWLEDGEMENTS

Thanks are due to the following: Frances Brown for help with the Bernands' French commentary on Julia Balbilla and for her excellent proofing; Stephen and Daphne Males for help with biblical references in Proba; the staff of the Joint Library of the Hellenic and Roman Societies, Institute of Classical Studies, London, for their courteous, informed and efficient help finding texts and commentaries; the staff of East Sussex County Library, Crowborough, for chasing books through Inter-Library Loan; my agent Carol Heaton for her tireless commit-ment and effort on behalf of the book; Jay and Trish Thompson for encouragement when most needed; to my family, as always, and above all, to Paul Dunn for hours spent reading, proofing and editing the poems – for living them with me.

I would like to thank the Society of Authors for their Authors' Foundation Grant.

CONTENTS

INTRODUCTION

Women's Poetry, Women's Lives

> *A woman learning how to write – what a sword she'll wield!*
> School copy-book, third or fourth century BC

> *Heaven created the nine Muses, but Earth has raised nine more*
> *For her own...*
> Antipater of Thessalonica, *c.* AD 20.[1]

In the first century AD, Antipater of Thessalonica's enthusiasm for classical women's poetry was hardly excessive; apart from his nine earthly 'Muses' – Praxilla, Moero, Anyte, Myrtis, Erinna, Telesilla, Corinna, Nossis and Sappho – modern scholarship has unearthed the names of at least thirteen additional Greek women poets, while the Roman period yields another seven – twenty-nine names in all.[2] Yet today the question asked first about their poetry is not the customary 'is it worth reading?' (although that often comes later), but rather, 'is there any left to read?'

Here Tillie Olsen's dictum that 'we who write are survivors' has a material as well as a metaphorical resonance.[3] Twenty-nine women writers represent only a fraction of the classical male writers whose work (or existence) is still known – far less than Olsen's ratio of 'one in twelve' for modern literature. And of these twenty-nine, the work of only sixteen is extant, often fragmentary. Although with medieval monasteries for their protectors, it is perhaps surprising that the intense sensualism not only of Sappho, but of lesser-known writers such as Nossis or the two Sulpicias, has survived at all.[4]

Given widely accepted beliefs about the status of women in antiquity – that they were denied legal and political rights, barely educated and kept in almost 'oriental seclusion'[5] – a more pressing question might be how they came to be poets at all; how they learnt their craft, in what circumstances they wrote or performed, how they perceived their work, and how it was received by the male literary establishment.

---

[1] *A.P.* 9.26.

[2] Wright 1923: 322-23; Pomeroy, 1977: 54-55, 60, Snyder, 1989: 128. For a full list see table on page 131.

[3] Olsen, 1980: 39.

[4] Richlin, 1992: 138.

[5] Pomeroy, 1975: 58.

These are complex issues. The poetry collected here spans a millennium, from Sappho in *c*.620 BC to Eudocia in *c*.420 AD; generalising about the conditions in which it was created is rather like drawing broad suppositions about British poetry from *Palgrave's Golden Treasury*, or *The Oxford Book of English Verse*. In addition, there is a geographical dispersion, from Nossis in southern Italy to the West, and Moero and Eudocia in Byzantium to the East. Corinna's intensely localised poetry, celebrating the topography and mythology of her native Boeotia in central Greece, suggests that despite the apparent homogeneity of Graeco-Roman culture, such local distinctions were crucial.[6]

Women's lives, too, were subject to local and historical conditions, their roles ranging from the respected family partners of early Greece,[7] to the politically active women of the Hellenistic kingdoms,[8] or the spiritual teachers of Christian Rome.[9] Until recently, such diversity had been overlooked, with the disenfranchised and secluded wives of fifth century BC Athens taken as the norm. When Joanna Bankier collected work for her anthology, *Women Poets of the World*, she discovered that women writers flourished in 'decentralised cultures', but vanished under 'a strong centralised power' where poetry became a prestigious activity.[10] Athens' dearth of women writers, at a time when male literary culture was exploding, is significant; as Nancy Rabinowitz has noted, 'there were times and places more hospitable to women writers'.[11]

An example is Greece in the sixth and early fifth centuries BC, when women and men's spheres were sharply divided – with men concerned with battle, government and trade, and women, marriage, the home and children.[12] The evidence of Homer's epic poems suggests, however, that in aristocratic tribal society, women's roles were respected, rather than devalued, with women occupying a parallel, exclusive world – a world celebrated in Sappho's poetry with its own emotional, spiritual and literary concerns.[13]

The nature of poetic composition – oral rather than written and sung rather than spoken – also worked to women's advantage, often

---

[6] See Hallett, 1992: 56.

[7] See Penelope, Nausicaa and Arete in the *Odyssey*.

[8] For a resume of the evidence see Pomeroy, 1975: 125-31.

[9] See Proba Nos.98-99; Eudocia No.100.

[10] Interviewed by Sheryl St Germain (1985: 20).

[11] Rabinowitz & Richlin, 1993: 10.

[12] 'Go home and attend to your work, to your loom and spindle,' Hector tells his wife Andromache in the *Iliad*, 'war is the concern of men' (6.490-2).

[13] See Winkler, 1981; Stigers, 1981.

excluded from education and far more likely to be illiterate.[14] In such circumstances, it has been suggested, women participated in a 'widespread female oral tradition', with songs handed down from mother to daughter.[15] Yet poetry was also performed publically, before the entire community, at religious festivals or weddings, with the poet's 'I' expressing communal as well as personal concerns.[16] And as the individualism of aristocratic society gave way to the increasingly communal consciousness of the new democracies, women poets, too, began to speak for the community at large, as well as of their own exclusive concerns; Telesilla of Argos, for example, writing in the early-fifth century BC, celebrated military victories, although her extant work includes hymns to female deities such as Artemis, and appears to have had a predominantly female audience.[17] Praxilla, writing in the Greek city of Sicyon at about the same time, celebrated women's religious concerns but also wrote drinking-songs, sung at male drinking parties, giving rise to suggestions that she was a *hetaira* or prostitute.[18]

During the classical period, women's poetry almost completely disappears from view, to re-emerge, with a vengeance, in the Hellenistic cities of the third and second centuries BC, with many of the classical women poets deriving from this time. Interestingly, given Bankier's findings on the conditions for women's poetry, this was a period of decentralisation, with the Greek and eastern empire of Alexander the Great fragmenting into smaller kingdoms. Now women were offered new opportunities of education – and literacy – becoming professional artists, musicians, athletes and even obstetricians. And women poets, many of whom, like Aristodama of Smyrna, travelled from city to city to perform their work, were honoured as never before, rewarded for their skill by prizes, state decrees, even political rights.[19]

Ironically, some feminist scholars have seen such expanded opportunities as a double-edged sword. Marilyn Skinner, for instance, has argued that as women gained literacy in the 'unisex' education system of the Hellenistic period, women poets began to produce –

---

[14] But Susan Cole lists some evidence for women's literacy, if on a small scale, in the fifth century BC (1981: 223-28).

[15] Skinner, 1993: 135. Certainly Sappho's companions compose songs together (see LP 22 & 96 / Balmer, Nos.22 & 33), and Sappho No.3 (LP 98) links the memories of mothers and daughters.

[16] See Slings, 1990: 3-7.

[17] See No.35 & p.49.

[18] See No.41 & p.53.

[19] See Pomeroy, 1977: 54-55.

and publish – poems for a predominantly male audience, exchanging the 'women-orientated' concerns of earlier eras, for a parroting of patriarchal values.[20] And alongside a new women's literacy, she sees a new denigration of women's work, with Sappho lampooned for sexual deviance for the first time.[21]

Against this can be set the praise of Antipater of Thessalonica quoted above, or the six epigrams in the Greek anthology celebrating Erinna's work, and the many imitations by male poets of Anyte's poems.[22] In addition, new opportunities for education, as well as the change from an oral to literate society, gave women poets the opportunity to study – and imitate – the work of their literary foremothers like Sappho, whom Erinna or Nossis, amongst others, continually echo.[23] As a result, a new confidence emerged – a consciousness of writing as women, in a tradition of women's poetry, which apparently continued (although the evidence is less plentiful) into the Roman era.[24]

The recitation of personal names is central here. Although both Sappho and Corinna name themselves in their poetry, it is the later poets who use their own names as a poetic trope, a recurrent battle-cry,[25] either to establish or celebrate their literary aims, as Nossis does in Nos.72, 79 & 83, or to assert, like Sulpicia, their equality in sexual love – and its literature (No.88); to leave an indelible mark on history, a recording of status and skill, as Julia Balbilla did on the stones of Egypt (Nos.95 & 97), or for the declaration of a spiritual, and literary, vocation in Proba's cento (No.98). The Roman satirist Juvenal might have sneered at 'the clattering talk' of literary – and literate – women, but the women poets themselves didn't balk at the sound of their own voices.[26]

---

[20] Skinner, 1983: 16-18.

[21] As were Erinna and Nossis (see Herodas, *Mimes*, 6 & p.83).

[22] *A.P.* 7.11-13, 9.190, 11.322; for Anyte see p.68.

[23] See Skinner, 1989; Rauk, 1989; Nos.42, 72, 79 & 83.

[24] For example, Sulpicia the Satirist's confident sensualism appears to echo that of the earlier Sulpicia (see Richlin, 1992: 138 & p.104).

[25] In 'The Distaff', Erinna uses Baucis' name as a cry of lament (see No.42, note 15), although her own name appears, in an uncertain context, later in the damaged text.

[26] *Satires*, 6.441. Myriam Diaz-Diocaretz has pointed to the importance of Adrienne Rich's use of her own name in her poetry, as 'a challenge' to both present and past conventions about poetic persona (1985: 102).

Women's Poems, Women's Poetry

Such confidence notwithstanding, how far is it possible to speak of a 'women's poetry' in the classical world? This is a contentious issue even for contemporary women poets, as an article by Germaine Greer – and the responses to it – have shown.[27] Certainly critical attitudes to women's poetry, both ancient and modern, have often been constant, reading art as biography, artifice as chance, artistic trademarks as gauche quirks.[28] Some poetic genres, too, are dismissed as more suitable for women – the short lyric or the playful epigram, dashed off between more pressing domestic duties,[29] while epic and didactic poetry are seen as predominantly male domains.

The poetry translated here does provide some remarkable correspondences. Images and themes, for instance, recur again and again: childhood games and memories (Nos.42, 60 & 117); the Muses (Nos. 6, 9, 14, 16 & 83); the moon (Nos.39 & 42); marriage (Nos.5, 42, 43 & 52); animals (Nos.7 & 61-63), women's work (Nos.42, 107-08 & 115), women's beauty (Nos.46 & 73-76), motherhood and women's generations (Nos.3, 50-51, 77, 79 & 102-05) women's deities such as Artemis (Nos.8, 35 & 82) or Aphrodite (Nos.58 & 73), women's festivals (Nos.39 & 113-14), lament (Nos.42-45,50-53 & 101-05) and last, but by no means least, love (Nos.1-2, 71-72, 85-93 & 110).[30]

Significantly, such themes still concern women poets today. In a recent anthology by the Poetry Book Society, half of the twenty or so poems by women (out of a total of about a hundred and fifty – only slightly better than Olsen's 'one in twelve') echo the above themes, from Stevie Smith's pet dog in 'Heartless' to Kathleen Raine's 'For the Bride' or Wendy Cope and Carol Ann Duffy's childhood memories in 'Tich Miller' and 'The Race' respectively.[31] Similarly, in Linda France's 1993 compilation, *Sixty Women Poets*, muses, moons, mothers and memories drift through the pages.

---

[27] Greer, 1995.

[28] For a comparison of attitudes to Sappho and Emily Brontë, for example, see Lefkowitz, 1981.

[29] For example, Jean-Jacques Rousseau: 'they can succeed in certain short works which demand only lightness, taste, grace' (quoted & translated by Kamuf, 1980: 290). Sarah Pomeroy comments that Hellenistic women writers thrived because of the period's taste for shorter, personal pieces which women, without privacy or time to study, could produce (1977: 56). However, the evidence of Erinna (No.42), Moero (No.47) and Proba (Nos.98-99), all extracts from epic poems, suggests that women could and did write substantial works. Many of the poets translated here also exhibit a high degree of learning and scholarship.

[30] See Elizabeth Bartlett's poem 'Themes for women' (France, 1993: 48-49).

[31] Barker, 1988: 25; 97; 180-81.

This emphasis on the personal and the domestic, on the startling epiphanies to be found within the everyday, has led both ancient and contemporary women's poetry to be dismissed as 'banal' or 'trivial', and perhaps worst of all, 'charming'.[32] Yet just as Stevie Smith's sad and sinister 'Heartless' promises far more than a simple tribute to her 'little dog', so Anyte's lament for her lost puppy (No.61) or Nossis' references to Thaumareta's guard-dog (No.75) conceal serious designs.[33] Both use the heroic language of Homer's epic verse – the archetype for the Greek male literary tradition – slyly subverting its conventions, applying its grandiose compound adjectives, normally reserved for battle-heroes, to household pets. In the process, they not only elevate the domestic to the heroic, but demote the heroic to the domestic, puncturing its pretensions, and merging 'high' and 'low' art forms. Although such techniques are typical of the Hellenistic era, which emphasised the equality of 'lesser' poetic forms,[34] their use by women poets, so often trapped by both demands and accusations of 'domesticity', has an added frisson.

Subversion of male literary forms is a constant throughout classical women's poetry. From Sappho's re-reading of the *Iliad*, in No.4,[35] to Proba's re-working of the *Aeneid* as a Christian epic,[36] far from aping the concerns of the prevailing patriarchy, as Skinner claims, women uncovered their own art within established genres, often re-shaping male literary forms, as Sappho transformed the personal lyric and Anyte the pastoral epigram. Even Corinna's localised myths, for which Marilyn Skinner reserves particular scorn, appear to offer subverted readings of traditional mythology, with topography replacing gender as the mechanism for dissent.[37]

Such revisionist myth-making has long been important to women's poets – 'the thieves of language', as Alicia Ostriker has named them.[38] Alongside this, one can set the recurrent use of memory in classical women's poetry, which assumes a poetic intensity, establishing both a personal and communal mythology, in which Corinna's folk-tales have the same intensity as Sappho's sensual remembrance of Anac-

---

[32] Balmer, 1992: 20-21; compare a male reviewer's dismissal of Amy Clampitt's 'fondness for accessorising detail' and of her measured, sombre verse as 'coy and cute'.

[33] See Ingrid Jonker's 'Dog', an Afrikaans poem which explores the tensions of apartheid through the metaphor of a chained hound (in Cosman, 1978: 310-11).

[34] See Nossis' epigram on the burlesque-writer, Rhinthon (No.80).

[35] See pp.23-24.

[36] Nos.98-99.

[37] See p.34-35.

[38] Ostriker, 1986. See Hedyle's 'Scylla' (No.71) & p.81, note 7.

toria or Erinna's re-telling of her childhood games with Baucis.[39] These poems, which existed both inside and outside the literary mainstream, recorded, reflected and also revised individual, collective and communal memories. Not surprisingly, they often articulate the tensions inherent in such a task – between male and female sexuality (Sappho and the two Sulpicias), male and female cultures (Telesilla and Praxilla), between Greek and Roman culture (Melinno), high and low art (Nossis and Anyte) or pagan and Christian spirituality (Proba and Eudocia); tensions often couched in humour or linguistic ambiguities.[40] Here, if anywhere, perhaps, is the special distinctiveness of 'classical women's poetry'.

Women's Poetry, Women's Language

If thematic and functional similarities can be traced in the work of classical women poets, what of semantic correspondences? The issue of 'women's language' is a thorny one, with battle-lines drawn up on all sides. On the one hand, feminist theorists such as Hélène Cixous, and Luce Irigaray consider women excluded from all 'phallogocentric' language structures, thus denying the historical existence of 'women's writing' as an identifiable genre with its own recognisable characteristics, while looking towards a utopian *écriture féminine* based on constructs of female sexuality. On the other, socio-linguists believe that language use is defined by gender, identifying specific female patterns and usages, or 'genderlects' within a given language.[41]

Recent scholarship on classical women's poetry has tended towards the theoretical approach, viewing 'woman' in classical literature as no more than a male construct, and the female voice of women's poetry, by extension, 'a male voice with a slight foreign inflection'.[42] Yet some studies have seen the private, segregated world of Sappho's poetry, in particular, as a forerunner of *écriture féminine*, offering an exploration of female sexuality, couched in exclusively female language and structures.[43]

---

[39] Corinna No.11, Sappho No.4; Erinna No.42.

[40] See Carol Ann Duffy's 'Litany', which articulates collective memory, implicitly rather than explicitly gender-defined, through an exploration of personal incident, while bristling with humour and sexual tension (1993: 9).

[41] See Cixous, 1976; McConnell-Ginet, 1980: 3-25; Tannen, 1995.

[42] Skinner, 1993: 129.

[43] Snyder, 1989: 21 & 1991: 13; Skinner, 1993; Winkler, 1981.

Ironically, this position has been held in the past by those classical scholars seeking to devalue women's poetry. In 1913, for example, Kirby Flower Smith bewailed Sulpicia's 'distinctly feminine' style, which rendered her Latin – an 'exclusively masculine' language – impossible to follow.[44] Smith's comments might have an historical basis; Cicero noted that aristocratic Roman women used specifically 'female' archaic expressions, and recent studies have suggested that the characters in Plautus' comic plays, too, use different linguistic forms, dependent on their gender.[45]

In translating the poets here, too, certain patterns began to emerge. Although it is often claimed that work by women poets is less 'crafted' than that of men,[46] over and over again they exhibited a fondness – and agility – for word-play, punning and neologism, all strategies adopted by writers like Cixous and Irigaray for their *écriture féminine*.[47] Similarly, rhyme, both end and internal, as well as alliteration, were widespread. And rather than the flashier metaphorical tropes of classical male poetry, the women poets create complex thematic patternings by the use of an apparently simplistic vocabulary, loading their words – as the small and therefore flexible lexicon of classical languages allows – with several layers of meaning.[48]

Another distinctive speech-form used by the women poets is dialect, from Sappho's Aeolic and Corinna's Boeotian forms to the highly artificial literary mélange of Erinna, Melinno or Julia Balbilla, superimposing Sappho's forms on their own.[49] This linguistic borrowing is at the heart of their art; not only do key words recur over and over – *teuchein*, 'to weave or create,' for example,

---

[44] Flower Smith: 81.

[45] See Lowe, 1988: 195 & further discussion on pp.95-97. Interestingly, the discovery of letters by both men and women at Vindolanda on Hadrian's Wall revealed a gender difference not in style, content or structure, but handwriting (Bowman, 1994: 124). Skinner also identifies a 'gender-specific speech trait' in Nossis' poetry, see No.79 & p.84.

[46] Snyder, 1989: 154; Bogin, 1980: 13.

[47] Suzanne Jill Levine has pointed out that puns, in particular, are the 'exile's tool', offering a 'binary view of...language and culture...both one's own and the other' (1991: 17).

[48] For example, in No.85, a declaration of love for Cerinthus, as well as weaving words of revelation and concealment throughout the poem, Sulpicia uses the verbs *deponere*, 'to set down', *exorare*, 'to prevail', or *mandare*, 'to entrust', which all have legal overtones – implicitly, rather than explicitly, creating a legal metaphor for her love-affair.

[49] Dialect is also an important feature in contemporary women's poetry. See the work of Kathleen Jamie.

or *tiktein*, 'to give birth'[50] – but certain conscious reference points are established between the poets' work; Sappho's use of the verb form *eba* from *bainein*, 'to leave' or 'sail away', a constant in Homer, to describe – and reinvent – Helen's desertion of Menelaus, for instance, appears in Anyte's lament for Philainis, another rewriting, this time of the sepulchral epitaph.[51] This is neither an exclusive *écriture féminine* or an identifiable 'genderlect' but the conscious creation of a parallel literary tradition, appropriating male literary forms, and investing Sappho as a female Homer – the semantic touchstone for all subsequent female artists.

Women in Translation

How, then, to transform such subtleties into another language, another culture? In translating Adrienne Rich's specifically lesbian poetry into Spanish – a language which marks gender and a culture which strictly defines it – Myriam Diaz-Diocaretz found it 'necessary to understand the poet's tradition, her "voice", and the different preoccupations reflected in her own world vision'.[52] By studying Rich's complete corpus, her statements about her work and through corresponding with the author, Diaz-Diocaretz was then able to choose or reject translations on the basis of Rich's own intentions.[53]

With classical works, not only have the textual intentions of their original writers been lost, but also most of the texts themselves. Far from uncovering the 'world-view' of many of the poets translated here, debate centres on where or when in the world, even if, they might have lived – with estimates sometimes varying by centuries.[54] In addition, the conditions for the creation, circulation and reception of classical poetry are mostly alien to a contemporary

---

[50] E.g. Nossis No.77, Anyte No.63; Sappho No.8, Corinna No.9, Nossis No. 83; see Adrienne Rich's poem 'Translations' in which the work of another woman poet is identified by the recurrent words: 'enemy, oven, sorrow' (1984: 169).

[51] See Nos. 4 & 50. The same verb has been conjectured for Baucis' desertion of Erinna in a missing piece of the papyrus of 'The Distaff' (see No.42, note 20).

[52] Diaz-Diocaretz, 1985: 40.

[53] See ibid: 126ff. Similarly, Tess O'Dwyer translated Giannina Braschi's prose-poem *Empire of Dreams* by reviewing Braschi's rejected first drafts, while Braschi worked simultaneously on O'Dwyer's English versions (Braschi/O'Dwyer, 1994: xix).

[54] See Corinna p.33; Erinna p.57, note 2; Melinno p.93; Sulpicia p.95.

17

audience; its oral composition and performance, the emphasis on tradition and reference, both literary and mythological, rather than originality or technical innovation, and a musical versification based not on stress but syllable length, all add to the difficulties of finding suitable equivalents. While Diaz-Diocaretz's commitment to the integrity of the text is a worthy role-model, clearly other strategies are required.

In the absence of a collaborative author, where can the translator of classical women's poetry look for guidance? One answer is to the work of contemporary women poets writing in English, whose linguistic nuances can resonate retrospectively in their literary foremothers; for by translating classical poetry into present-day English, it becomes at once ancient and modern, the product of both an unknown and familiar culture. In 'The Distaff', for example (No.42), Erinna invokes the mythic female figure Mormo, usually described as a 'female bugaboo' or 'bogie', although with her counterpart Empusa, she was also characterised in Greek literature as a beautiful and/or sexually insatiable woman.[55] Looking for a descriptive noun which admitted these ancient gender assumptions but omitted any superfluous modern condescension, I came across two lines in Adrienne Rich's poem 'Planetarium': 'A woman in the shape of a monster/a monster in the shape of a woman.' These, in turn, echoed May Sarton's call to 'we who are writing women and strange monsters':[56] Mormo the monster, fortuitously alliterative, had arrived.

This example raises other problems: how far should the translated text explain or expand culturally specific references in the original? In translating Rich's poem, 'Pierrot le Fou', Diaz-Diocaretz agonised over a reference to the New York district of the Bowery – not just a topographical name but also 'a composite series of images' for American readers.

Eventually, she decided on elaboration: *the Bowery, la calle de los borrachos* ('the Bowery, the street of the drunks').[57] Such dilemmas occur over and over in classical poetry; in an epigram by Anyte, for example, she calls the slayer of a pet cicada 'Sinis' after a mythological thief whose name became proverbial in Greek (No.62). I transformed him into 'Robbie the Ravager' to emphasise Anyte's teasing mock-heroics, as well as both her proverbial and proper

---

[55] Snyder, 1989: 95; Rayor, 1991: 187; Aristophanes, *Frogs*, 289ff.

[56] Rich, 1984: 114; Sarton, 'My Sisters, O My Sisters'. However, occasionally it was suitable to use male writers for models, as, for example, in Praxilla's 'male' drinking songs (see No.41, (ii), note 15).

[57] Diaz-Diocaretz, 1985: 144.

usage. Here, too, are further acts of collaboration – between women in translation and women translators.

Suzanne Jill Levine's deft and witty solutions to salvaging, in English, Manuel Puig's or Guillermo Cabrera Infante's complex Spanish puns, were also an inspiration. Faced with Puig's character Dr Aschero in his novel *Boquitas pintadas* ('Heartbreak Tango'), she scoured phone books and came up with 'Dr Nasti' (*asco* = 'nausea'), later further transformed to 'Dr Nastini' to echo Aschero's Italian immigrant origins.[58] Similarly, a fragment by Erinna, apparently part of a lament for her dead friend Baucis, addresses *Pompilos*, the 'escort-fish', punning on the Greek verbs, *pempein*, 'to send' and *pompeuein* 'to escort' (No.44). I called him 'Solonicus', a sole guide, and soul escort, opening up further possibilities for punning on the loneliness of Baucis' last journey, while retaining the alliteration of the Greek.[59]

These devices offer a mimetic, rather than strictly semantic, 'faithful' translation, with the aim, as Octavio Paz has noted, of reproducing the effect by changing the text.[60] Elsewhere, it was not always possible to find such direct correspondences, in which case I was guided by the poet's general strategies. For example, Anyte's recurrent use of internal rhyme and alliteration became a spring-board for translating her poetry, even if my usage didn't always directly correspond with hers. Again, Sulpicia's Latin word-play and sensual innuendo provided a blueprint for my English; sometimes our paths crossed (*cum de me cogitat, ille calet /* 'you turn his thoughts to mine, make his body yearn for mine'),[61] occasionally I had to abandon her breathtaking concision in one line to graft it onto another.

Sulpicia's poetry introduced another dilemma; to rhyme or not to rhyme. Like Anyte, she makes use of end rhyme, yet somehow the spectre of nineteenth-century poesy, or even Pope's *Iliad*, hangs over rhymed classical translations. With women's poetry there is an additional problem – rhyme is often seen as a device of 'low' or 'frivolous' art; by employing it, my translations could well trivialise their art. On the other hand, contemporary women poets such as Stevie Smith or Wendy Cope have explored its potential with style,

---

[58] Levine, 1991: 62.

[59] Compare Sulpicia No.89, note 32.

[60] Honig, 1985: 155. Paz points to Pierre Leiris' French translations of T.S. Eliot where 'In the room the women come and go/Talking of Michelangelo' became 'Dans le salon les femmes vont et viennent/en parlant des maîtres de Sienne'.

[61] No.91.

and I therefore decided to follow their lead.[62] Alien classical metres and forms pose another problem. Influenced by poets like Marianne Moore, I decided to adopt a syllable count to stand in for the 'syllable-value' (long or short) of ancient versification.

Such devices could lead to the accusation of 'over-translation'. As Edmund Keeley observed of Cavafy, there is the danger of 'jazzing-up' poetry which might otherwise appear flat.[63] This is a particular problem with early poetry, originally performed to musical accompaniment, which, like song lyrics, can seem disappointing on the page.[64] Such tampering might appear as cultural arrogance, casting the freshness of classical poetry as 'inferior' to the more tortuous semantic complexities of modern (and particularly modernist) poetry. In the case of women poets, there is also the danger of implying – as has often been the case – an ineptitude based on gender.

Yet fragmentary poetry can be frustrating for the reader – how can the translator persuade them that a string of seemingly unconnected lines is worth their attention? In the past, classical translators often solved this problem by reconstructing as they translated, a practice now frowned upon, although, with the rise of deconstructive techniques, perhaps ripe for a renaissance. In *Classical Women Poets*, I have followed the prevailing orthodoxy (except where editors' emendations to the Greek text have become standard). As Diane Rayor has noted, fragments can also offer intriguing possibilities, echoing broken conversations, trailing voices.[65] In 'The Distaff', for example, the papyrus has frayed away just as the text read *druptei* or 'tears'; this suggested the form of my version, a series of fragmented memories, falling across the page.

But what of a string of words? Or even a single word? How can they be rendered as poetry? In both *Sappho: Poems and Fragments* and here, I adopted the strategy of grouping fragments by theme, although this is of necessity a highly subjective task, reliant on individual readings of ambiguous texts. Even more subjectively, I strung together stray words or quotations into a single piece, as for example Corinna No.25 or Telesilla No.35. Here, I was often guided by the framing of the texts; by additional information pro-

---

[62] Michael Longley's use of rhyme in his poem, 'Ceasefire', a transformation of Homer's *Iliad* against a sub-text of contemporary Belfast politics, has shown that it can have an affecting place in the deeply serious poetry of grief and loss: ' "I get down on my knees and do what must be done/And kiss Achilles' hand, the killer of my son" ' (Longley, 1995: 39). See Anyte Nos. 50-51.

[63] Honig, 1985: 143.

[64] See Robert Fitzgerald on translating Homer, ibid: 110.

[65] Rayor, 1990: 17.

vided by the classical commentators who preserved them, such as poem titles or mythological explanations. Sometimes, this frame became part of the poem itself, as in Corinna No.28, where alternative versions recorded by a grammarian were incorporated within the translation. And where I had earlier rejected the strategy of titling translations (in *Sappho: Poems and Fragments* I had employed titled sections instead), I decided to adopt it here, again guided by and sometimes incorporating commentators' records of the text, as well as modern readings.[66]

Another problem was the variety of voices contained here – not one, as with Sappho, but sixteen distinct, highly idiosyncratic styles. With each one speaking now in my own voice, as well as their own, how far was it possible to convey that difference?[67] How far, too, should accepted judgements of relative literary worth be considered, judgements which place Sappho at the top of the literary pantheon, and Julia Balbilla or Melinno firmly at its base? The answer lay in the poets themselves; their voices, I discovered, were far too strong to be ignored. And as I became more intimate with their works, I found qualities to admire even in the most derided of writers. Although anxious not to overwork the texts, I adopted the policy of playing to their strengths, so that Balbilla's internal rhymes and succinct phrasing, for example, more than compensated for any technical roughness.[68]

All these decisions were guided by one force: poetry – the desire to make poems from a lost culture and in dead languages live once again in ours. Carol Maier has complained that this process of translation is often perceived as 'a task that does not occur in the realms of thought but between the pages of a dictionary.'[69] Yet over and over it was necessary to refer to scholarly interpretations of damaged or ambiguous texts in order to tease out both meaning and artistry. The final lines of Erinna's poem 'The Distaff', for example, have been variously interpreted by scholars; my own reading – and translation – attempts to admit their theories but was guided most of all by the need to retain the ambiguity of the original poem.[70]

---

[66] On the issue of adding titles to classical translations, see Barnstone, 1985: 11.

[67] As Carol Maier has noted of translating Octavio Armand: 'I know that it is his tongue but I know also that it is mine and I know that it would not be speaking in English if our two tongues were in perfect accord' (1985: 7).

[68] See p.107ff.

[69] Maier, 1986: 25.

[70] See No.42, note 21.

These techniques occasion the need for another: the footnote. Barbara Godard has exhorted fellow translators to 'flaunt' their presence by the use of such notes.[71] With *Sappho: Poems and Fragments*, I had restricted these to the mythological or historical, to cultural references in the text which could best be captured by external rather than internal expansion. Here, I have also included a commentary on many of the processes of translating, recording the original's textual strategies alongside those of my translation, wherever possible, on the basis that if different strategies were being employed the reader should be kept as informed as possible. My purpose was to help monolingual as well as bilingual readers, to give them the experience of comparison, of judgement more normally reserved for the scholar.[72]

Such devices aim to free both reader and translation from the illusion that reading these poems is the same act as reading their originals; to throw off, with Sulpicia, the shackles of feminine 'fidelity'. And like Sulpicia's witty and above all assured missives to Cerinthus, these translations, too, are teasing, loving, occasionally frustrated, sometimes straying but always striving for equality – a razor-sharp sword to reassert their concerns, their own voices.

Their very presence.

JOSEPHINE BALMER

KEY TO THE TRANSLATIONS:

[ ]   denotes a conjectural meaning
...   denotes a break in the papyrus
*   denotes the end of a fragment

---

[71] Godard, 1990: 89-96.

[72] As Susan Bassnett suggests, when Dryden, Jonson or Pope translated classical works, their small, aristocratic and highly literate audiences were familiar with the originals, allowing the translator more freedom to play with the source text – a play their readers could recognise and enjoy – which often resulted in more 'successful' translations (Bassnett, 1991: 90).

SAPPHO

Sappho, the most revered of all classical women poets, lived in the city of Mytilene on Lesbos, an island off the coast of Asia Minor, around 600 BC. About two hundred fragments of her lyric poems survive,[1] although little is known of her life. However, a few of her poems refer to the struggle for power between aristocratic factions in Mytilene, suggesting she was a member of the wealthy ruling-class.[2] Apart from this her poetry, as Joan DeJean has recently noted, relegates men to a peripheral role, and is concerned almost exclusively with women – their family relationships, their religious festivals and female deities, particularly Aphrodite, and most of all, their intense emotional relationships.[3]

Such relationships have obsessed studies of her work throughout the ages, from the salacious gossip of Greek comic playwrights to Victorian gentleman scholars. This century, Freudians, feminists and philologists have all argued about her sexuality, poring over her fragmentary poems as if they were a biographical tract.[4] In 1913, one German scholar postulated that Sappho was the 'head-mistress' of a school of girls on Lesbos, dedicated to the cult of Aphrodite, and her most intense declaration of sensual desire (No.2), was a wedding-hymn for a favourite 'pupil'.[5] In 1979 the feminist scholar Judith Hallett also claimed that Sappho held a 'formal' position on Lesbos, with her poetry acting as 'a sensual conscious-ness-raiser' for segregated young girls 'on the threshold of marriage and maturity'.[6] The debate over her sexuality still rages, with some scholars convinced of Sappho's lesbianism, others concentrating on a more emotional sensuality.[7]

More productive is the study of Sappho's poetic concerns, examining how she establishes an alternative world in which a set of female values are asserted in direct opposition to those of male culture. In No.4, for example, she asks the question 'what is the loveliest sight on earth?' and after rejecting armies, cavalries or fleets – the male forces of war – she answers it, 'whatever you desire,'

---

[1] Translated in Balmer, 1992.
[2] 71 LP / Balmer: No.46; 155 LP / Balmer: 45.
[3] DeJean, 1987: 790.
[4] See Lefkowitz, 1981a: 59–68.
[5] Wilamowitz, 1913: 56ff.
[6] Hallett, 1979: 450.
[7] Winkler, 1981; Stigers, 1979; Snyder, 1991.

using the example of Helen's desertion of Menelaus for Paris of Troy to prove the point. But whereas in Homer's *Iliad*, Helen is a passive figure stolen away like an inanimate object to live in misery and regret in Troy until reclaimed by the Greeks as a prize of war, Sappho's Helen acts of her own free will, motivated only by desire.[8] In a direct echo of a passage from Homer, where Helen weeps as she remembers the home and family she has left behind, Sappho has her Helen care nothing for her husband, child or parents, transforming her from a puppet of kings into a decisive woman, forsaking her traditional role as daughter, wife and mother for the demands of her own sexuality.[9]

Over and over again in Sappho's poetry she rewrites male literary tradition, replacing it with a parallel female value-system. In Hesiod's epic poetry, for example, marriage is depicted as an evil, with women a burden, 'a bane to mortal men'.[10] In Sappho's wedding songs, she reasserts both the qualities of the bride, and the good-fortune of the groom, who relishes, rather than fears, his change of status.[11] Similarly, a recent study by Eva Stigers has shown how Sappho subverts erotic male poetry, overturning its emphasis on domination and submission to find metaphors based on 'female biology and psychology'; where Anacreon characterises his male lover as a charioteer, holding the reins to his soul, for example, Sappho portrays her beloved, Atthis, as a tiny child.[12] Important here, too, is Sappho's constant expression of memory and loss, whether for the past pleasure of Anactoria's 'radiant, sparkling face' (No.4) or the luxuries of her youth (No.3), asserting the value of individual women and establishing a collective history.[13]

But most of all, Sappho transformed the lyric genre, a new form of personal literary expression replacing – as well as subverting – Homer's epic poems. Ancient commentators record that Sappho invented many analogies which later became commonplace: the moon as 'silver', for example, a reflection of the growing use of coinage, or love as 'bittersweet'.[14] To jaded modern palates, the

---

[8] *Iliad* 3.173-76; 6.344-48; 24.762-75; see duBois, 1978; Balmer, 1992: 22-23.

[9] For a comparison of this poem with other male versions of the myth, see Balmer, ibid: 22.

[10] Hesiod, *Theogony*, 567-612; *Works & Days:* 54-105.

[11] See No.5.

[12] Stigers, 1981: 50-52; Anacreon 15; Sappho 49 LP / Balmer, No.35. See No.1 (iii).

[13] For a further discussion of the importance of memory in classical women's poetry, see Introduction pp-14-15.

[14] See 34 LP / Balmer, No.112; No.1 (II).

freshness of such poetry, its directness and vigour, can easily be overlooked. Yet its intensity burned thoughout antiquity, still influencing poetic declarations of emotion over five hundred years later when the Latin male poet Catullus imitated her work.[15]

But Sappho's poetry also spoke for her community, for the women she addresses in her poems, who listened and composed alongside her.[16] To the later classical women poets, too, her poems were a source of inspiration, borrowed, imitated and honoured in their own work, links in a chain which stretched from Nossis and Erinna in the third century BC to Julia Balbilla in the second AD – and beyond to H.D., May Sarton, and Adrienne Rich in our own.[17]

The following selection is taken from my earlier collection, *Sappho: Poems and Fragments*,[18] which offers a full translation of her work. The final poem, however, is included here for the first time, formerly attributed to Sappho's male contemporary, Alcaeus, but restored to her by a recent edition.[19]

---

[15] Catullus 51; see No.2.
[16] See 22 LP / Balmer, No.22: 'I beg you, Gongyla,/take up your lyre and sing to us.'
[17] See Introduction p.16-17.
[18] Balmer, Bloodaxe Books, 1992.
[19] LP 304; Campbell, 1982: No.44a.

1: Love

I

                            Love shook my heart
like the wind on the mountain
rushing over the oak trees

*

II

Love makes me tremble yet again
                  sapping all the strength from my limbs;

bittersweet,[20] undefeated creature –
                  against you there is no defence[21]

*

III [22]

[I ran after you]
like a small child
              flying
                      to her mother

---

[20] **bittersweet**: Nossis imitates Sappho's imagery here in No.72.

[21] **undefeated...no defence**: The use of military images in a romantic context became a constant in classical poetry, but Sappho was one of the first poets to transpose the language of epic conflicts to a more personal battleground. Here, the startling effect of the single Greek adjective, *amachanos* ('unconquerable'), is emphasised by repetition in English.

[22] This fragment is attributed to either Sappho or her male contemporary, Alcaeus (LP i.a.25), although usually ascribed to Sappho; its mother/child imagery strongly suggests Sappho's authorship – a common feature in her poetry (see LP 49 / Balmer 35; LP 132 / Balmer 75 & LP 122 / Balmer 77 & p.24 above).

2: Desire

It seems to me that man is equal to the gods,[23]
that is, whoever sits opposite you
and, drawing nearer, savours, as you speak,
the sweetness of your voice

and the thrill of your laugh, which have so stirred the heart
in my own breast, that whenever I catch
sight of you, even if for a moment,
then my voice deserts me

and my tongue is struck silent, a delicate fire
suddenly races underneath my skin,
my eyes see nothing, my ears whistle like
the whirling of a top

and sweat pours down me and a trembling creeps over
my whole body, I am greener than grass;[24]
at such times I seem to be no more than
a step away from death;[25]

but all can be endured since even a pauper...

---

[23] **That man**: Several interpretations of this poem have seen the male figure as its focus, either as the husband of one of Sappho's pupils, or the rival lover of one of her companions, even reading in it 'a clinically commonplace female castration complex' (Devereux, 1970: 22). However, the focal point here is neither man nor woman, but the object of desire, the violent emotions aroused by the physical presence of that object. Sappho's use of the verb form *phainetai* 'it seems', emphasises the indefinite, illusory quality of such emotions, echoed in the translation here (see Lefkowitz, 1981a: 59-68).

[24] **greener than grass**: Sappho here uses the adjective *chloros*, which can mean both brilliant green and pale yellow. Some translators have rendered it as 'paler than grass', a reference to the colour draining from the speaker's face, or seen in it an expression of Sappho's clinical jealousy; Mary Lefkowitz (ibid) has noted that it could be an echo of Homer's 'green fear', which struck warriors in battle, with Sappho, again, transposing the male language of war to a context of female emotion, an interpretation I have followed (for *chloros*, see Irwin, 1974: 31ff). Anyte also uses the adjective ambiguously (Nos.50, 53, 55).

[25] **a step from death**: Sappho's description of the physical sensation of desire became a constant in later poetry (see Catullus 51 and Dido in Ovid's *Heroides*, 7.23-30), even influencing medical belief; a Hellenistic physician diagnosed a case of sexual obsession with reference to her poem (see Plutarch, *Life of Demetrius*, 38; Sulpicia, No.91, note 36).

3: Mother and Daughter [26]

...my mother [used to say that]
in her youth it was thought to be
very fine to bind up your hair

with a dark purple [headband] – yes
extremely fine indeed, although
for a girl whose hair is golden

like a torch-flame [better] to wreathe
in it garlands of fresh flowers;
recently [I saw] a headband,

brightly coloured, from Sardis... [27]
but for you, Cleis, [28] I do not have
a brightly coloured headband nor [29]
do I know where I may find one...

---

[26] **Mother and Daughter**: Three generations of women are the subject of
Nossis No.79, also grouped around an item of clothing – an offering for the
goddess Hera. The theme is a favourite, too, with many modern women poets,
for example, Ruth Fainlight's 'Choosing', centred on a hated childhood dress
(1994: 30), or Eléni Vakaló's modern Greek poem, 'Genealogy', which evokes
her grandmother through memories of a hat (in Cosman, 1978: 259, trans-
lated by Paul Merchant).

[27] **Sardis**: A city in the rich and powerful kingdom of Lydia on the main-
land of Asia Minor across the straits from Lesbos. Sappho juxtaposes its
wealth and luxury with the natural riches of her daughter's beauty (see LP
132 / Balmer No.75).

[28] **Cleis**: According to some ancient commentators, the name of both
Sappho's mother and her daughter.

[29] **brightly-coloured headband**: The repetition of the same words –
poikilan mitranan – throughout a relatively short poem (although a central
block of text is missing here) might jar on modern sensibilities, more accus-
tomed, in a literate age of reading and re-reading, to change and invention.
However, although *poikilos*, in particular, has several different resonances in
Greek – 'many-coloured', 'spotted' or 'finely-wrought' – I decided to echo
the Greek usage and repeat 'brightly-coloured' throughout, to emphasise the
contrast between the specific headband Sappho wishes for her daughter in
the present, with the putative purple band of the second stanza – an abstrac-
tion of the past, bound up with Sappho's memories of her mother. The oral
composition and performance of the poem, too, would favour such repetition.

4: Helen [30]

Some an army on horseback, some an army on foot
and some say a fleet of ships is the loveliest sight
on this dark earth; but I say it is what-
ever you desire:

and it is perfectly possible to make this clear
to all; for Helen, the woman who by far surpassed
all others in her beauty, left her husband –
the best of all men –

behind and sailed far away to Troy,[31] she did not spare
a single thought for her child nor for her dear parents
but [the goddess of love] led her astray
[to desire...]

　　　　　　　　　[...which]
reminds me now of Anactoria
although far away,

whose long-desired footstep, whose radiant, sparkling face
I would rather see before me than the chariots
of Lydia[32] or the armour of men
who fight wars on foot...

---

[30] **Helen**: For a full discussion of the mythological context of this poem see p.24.

[31] **sailed away**: Sappho's use of the Greek verb *bainein*, 'to leave or sail away', for desertion is echoed in Anyte No.50, and possibly, although the text is uncertain, in Erinna's 'Distaff' (No.42) of Baucis' death: see Introduction on p.17.

[32] **Lydia**: The kingdom of Lydia's great wealth, military might and power-ful trade links, here all symbolise the male concerns of archaic Greek society (see Introduction, p.10, note 12), which Sappho rejects for a sight of Anac-toria's face.

5: Marriage

Lucky bridegroom,[33]
the marriage you have prayed for has come to pass
and the bride you dreamed of is yours...

Beautiful bride,
to look at you gives joy; your eyes are like honey,
love flows over your gentle face...

Aphrodite
has honoured you above all others

6: Poetry and the Muses [34]

[Sappho said:]

The Muses have made me happy
in my lifetime

and when I die
I shall never be forgotten.[35]

---

[33] **Lucky bridegroom**: Here, in contrast to archaic Greek male poets, Sappho emphasises the fortune of men in marriage and the qualities of their bride (see p.24).

[34] **The Muses**: The nine goddesses of poetic inspiration. Invocations to the Muses are a constant in ancient – and modern – women's poetry, see Corinna, Nos. 10, 14, 27; Nossis, No.83; Proba, No.98; and Eavan Boland, 'The Muse Mother' (1989: 54); Elaine Feinstein, 'Muse' (in France, 1993: 139) & Anna Akhmatova, 'The Muse' (McKane, 1989: 114).

[35] **never be forgotten**: According to ancient commentators, Sappho was the first to say that poetry confers immortality on the poet.

7: The Evening Star [36]

Hesperus, you bring everything that
> the light-tinged dawn has scattered;

you bring the sheep, you bring the goat, you bring
> the child back to its mother

---

[36] **The Evening Star**: This poem is a forerunner of Anyte's pastoral epigrams (see Nos.54-56).

8: Artemis' Oath [37]

For golden-haired Apollo, whose life had been Leto's gift [38]
when she took Cronus' lofty son to bed – up-in-the-clouds
named-for-glory Zeus [39] – [there would be many, many lovers.]
But his sister Artemis swore an oath, the greatest oath
of the gods. 'On your head, father Zeus, I will be virgin
forever – unbedded, unbroken, following the hunt
on lonely peaks of untrodden mountains. So come, my Lord,
grant this one thing on my behalf.' These were Artemis' words.
And the father of the sacred gods nodded his assent.
So now both gods and men have named her Virgin, Deer-shooter,
Lover of the Chase [40] – solemn titles for a solemn oath.
And Desire, limb-trembler, heart-trapper, can never catch her. [41]

---

[37] **Artemis**: Sappho's poetry is often concerned with female deities, although more usually Aphrodite, the goddess of love. However, her work also refers to myths about women (142 & 166 LP / Balmer: Nos. 97 & 96), and the glory of virginity is a recurrent theme (e.g. LP 107 & 114 / Balmer, Nos.69-71). The presence of Artemis in a poem attributed to Nossis, who modelled her work on Sappho's, might suggest further evidence of Sappho's authorship (see No.82 & also Telesilla No.35).

[38] **Leto's gift**: Leto was the mother of Apollo and Artemis by Zeus. The form of the Greek verb *tiktein*, 'to produce' or 'give birth', that Sappho uses here is found in Homer of the father's role in fertilisation rather than that of the mother (*Iliad* 6.206). This translation emphasises Sappho's implicit insistence on women's role in birth.

[39] **Zeus...Cronus**: The myth of Zeus and his father Cronus is explored in Corinna No.10 and Moero No.47.

[40] **Lover of the Chase**: see Sulpicia's characterisation of Diana in No.92.

[41] **limb-trembler**: Campbell conjectures *lusimeles*, 'limb-shaker', a compound adjective also used by Sappho in the first line of No.1 (II), and employed of sleep in Homer (*Odyssey*, 20.57); here, I added an emphatic repeat, 'heart-trapper', to echo the implied tension between Artemis' lonely hunt, and 'the chase' of love – a tension which also reappears in Sulpicia No.92.

CORINNA

Corinna lived in the city of Tanagra in Boeotia, a district of central Greece. About forty fragments of her work survive, more than any classical woman poet except Sappho, ranging from single words to forty line narratives, although even these are incomplete. Like Sappho, her poetry appears to have been written for an audience of women, and in particular, as No.9. suggests, for female choruses to sing at religious festivals, focusing on local topography and variants of well-known myths, which are not found elsewhere.[1] Her style is also innovative, a blend of local dialect and 'high' poetic stylisms, drawn like Sappho's, from Homer, as well as from Sappho's own Aeolic forms, making a unique whole, half vernacular, half literary and rather more artificial than might at first appear.

To complicate matters further, although some ancient commentators claim she was a contemporary of Pindar, a Boeotian male poet of the fifth century BC (and that both were pupils of the poetess Myrtis whose work is now lost),[2] the distinctive spelling conventions found on the surviving manuscript of her work, the Berlin Papyrus, date from around the third century BC. An academic debate has ensued, with scholars lining up on both sides. Those who argue for the later date point out that Corinna's work seems to be unknown to other classical writers before the first century BC, when she was praised by the Roman poet Propertius and the Greek epigrammatist, Antipater of Thessalonica.[3] Those in favour of the earlier date counter that there is no strong reason to doubt the testimony of the sources, and that Corinna's work might well have been lost, then rediscovered and recopied around 200 BC.[4] In addition, the Christian writer Tatian describes a statue of Corinna by the fourth-century sculptor Silanion which, as Jane Snyder points out, would suggest that Corinna's reputation was established long before 200 BC.[5] Here, like other recent editions and studies of classical women's poetry,[6] I have placed Corinna in the fifth century, as the mythological subjects of her work appear to

---

[1] See Page 1953: 25.
[2] *Suda* K 2087; Plutarch *On the Glory of Athens* 4.347f-348a; Aelian *Historical Miscellanies*, 13.25; Pausanias, *Description of Greece*, 9.22.3.
[3] Propertius, *Elegies*, 2.3.21; *A.P.* ix.26; see Page 1953: 69 & West 1977.
[4] See Page 1953: 71 & Bowra 1931.
[5] Tatian, *Against the Greeks*, 52B; Snyder 1989: 44.
[6] See Snyder 1984 & 1989; Rayor 1991 & 1993.

have more in common with her near contemporaries Sappho, Tele-
silla and Praxilla than the more everyday themes of the Hellenistic
poets Erinna, Anyte and Nossis (although the third century frag-
ment of Hedyle could prove a closer match). However, as Page
comments, the arguments seem inconclusive on both sides.[7]

As well as Corinna's date, the merit of her work has long been
a cause of critical concern. The geographer Pausanias, who wrote
around 150 AD, noting the story that Corinna once defeated Pindar
in a poetic contest, comments that it must have been her beauty
which swayed the judges.[8] Modern scholarship has been even less
kind; Corinna's poetry, like that of Sappho and so many other women
poets, has often been accused of parochial homeliness and 'extreme
simplicity'. Feminist critics have been even harsher, charging Cor-
inna's often brutal mythologies of perpetrating a male-dominated
literary tradition – 'the male-value system' – within her female world.[9]

Corinna's impersonal narratives might seem distant to the mod-
ern reader. Yet, as we have seen, Corinna's verse is not without
artifice. As well as the use of Homeric compound adjectives to
create a heroic, universal context for her very localised stories,
Corinna employs more familiar poetic devices such as assonance,
alliteration and enjambment to add intensity and movement to her
verse. Through the use of a deceptively simple diction, she builds
a complex unity of language and theme, as, for example, in No.10,
where the human and geographical qualities of the two mountain
contestants are interwoven. And if ostensibly austere, her verse is
not without humour – witness the defeated Helicon's petulant
shower of stones, an echo of the pebbles which outvoted him.[10] As
for the charge of 'male-orientation', levelled particularly at No.112,
which appears to condone the abduction of Asopus' nameless
daughters, where other versions of the myth highlight Asopus'
anger and revenge at their theft as if his property,[11] Corinna
emphasises his grief and sense of loss – like Sappho's wedding
poems, insisting on the emotional value women might hold in a
society in which they were often dispensable bartering tools
between male family members. And if the poem resonates with
submission, as Snyder has suggested,[12] then it is not only that of

---

[7] Page 1953: 74.
[8] Pausanias, *Descripion of Greece*, 9.22.3.
[9] Snyder 1984: 130; Page 1953: 21; Skinner 1983: 10.
[10] See Rayor 1991: 182.
[11] See Pausanias 2.5.1; Apollodorus 3.12.6. See also Page 1953: 25.
[12] Snyder 1984: 130.

women to men, but of mortals to gods, reason to desire, offering the comfort of prestige in return for suffering in a world where even the art of prophecy is a trophy to be seized.

Such mythological concerns link, not distance, Corinna's poetry with that of Sappho, establishing a collective historical consciousness, a familiar world of memory. And if Corinna's concerns are communal rather than personal, with well-known local places and folk-tales taking the place of lovers and companions, her poems still resonate with the comfort of the past, the power of female tradition.[13]

---

[13] See Introduction pp.14-15.

9: Songs of Old [14]

On me my Muse has served her summons
to sing those beautiful songs of old
for Tanagran women in their dawn-
white dresses; as the city takes such
pleasure in my teasing-trilling [15] songs.

for whatever great [deeds great heroes
might perform,] still taller tales [are told,]
the earth their open field for battle.
And so I've reset our fathers' tales,
[reworked their crown with these new jewels]
as I take up my lyre for my girls:

Often I've polished tales of Cephisus, [16]
our country's own first founding-father,
often of Lord Orion, [17] the fifty
high-and-mighty sons he brought into
being – with help from their mother nymphs;

and then at last I sang of Libya, [18]
[Thebes' fair fore-mother…]

---

[14] **Songs of Old**: The title of this fragment has caused some problems of interpretation. The Greek word *Geroia*, of uncertain etymology, has sometimes been derived from a feminine form of *geron*, 'an old man' and translated as 'Old Wives Tales', which in English implies a judgement of merit not found in the original. Recently, Dee Clayman has suggested a derivation from the verb *eirein*, 'to speak' or 'narrate', pointing to the poem's statements of intent in evidence (Clayman, 1978). 'Songs of Old' admits both readings, takes in the verb *aeidein*, 'to sing', from line 2, but loses any suggestion of scorn.

[15] **teasing-trilling**: Corinna coins a new compound adjective here, *ligouro-kotilos*, whose precise meaning is unclear: *ligouros* means 'clear' or 'shrill', often used of a voice, while *kotilos* can mean 'chattering' or 'babbling', and in Theocritus' playfully misogynist fifteenth *Idyll*, 'gossiping' women (89), although the poet Anacreon uses it of a swallow (394a PMG). Page points to Hesiod's use of *kotilos* in *Works & Days* (374) of 'wheedling' or 'coaxing' women (1953: 30), a meaning I followed here – but without Hesiod's sense of censure.

[16] **Cephisus**: A river-god of Boeotia, and in local mythology, apparently Tanagra's founder.

[17] **Orion**: A giant hunter, and local god of Boeotia; after his death from a scorpion-bite, he was placed among the stars (see Nos.11, 20, 30 & Moero No.47, note 9).

10: The Contest of Cithaeron and Helicon [19]

[...And Cithaeron took up his lyre and sang:[20]
'Remember how] the Guardians of Zeus [21]
hid the immortal infant in a cave
with care, their fledgling secret, from crafty
crooked Cronos; for the mother goddess,
sacred Rhea, had stolen him away

and seized the gods' great renown for herself.'
So Cithaeron finished his final song.
Straight way the Muses served notice on the Gods
to place their pebbles, secret votes, in gold-
polished urns. And they all stood up at once.

But Cithaeron took the majority.
At once swift Hermes revealed the result:
Cithaeron had taken the victory
he had longed for, won honour for himself.
Then the gods ringed his brow with a garland
of pines; and his stony heart turned over.

As for the defeated, Helicon's prize
was a bitter envy; with a shudder
he tore out a smooth rock from his mountain-
side, and groaning in pain as the earth shook,
hurled it from on high, snowing a thousand
thousand pebbles on the lands far below...

---

[18] **Libya**: A little-known nymph, daughter of Cassiopeia. Campbell suggests she might have been an ancestor of Cadmus who founded the city of Thebes (1992: 37).

[19] **Cithaeron & Helicon**: Mountains in Boeotia, both sacred to the Muses, and here contestants in a singing-contest judged by the gods. Snyder points out such contests are a common motif in modern Greek folk-literature (1989: 46).

[20] As the fragment begins, Cithaeron is ending his song; the content of Helicon's song has been lost.

[21] **Zeus**: Cithaeron tells the legend of Zeus' childhood: jealous of his children, Zeus' father, Cronos, swallowed them at birth, but Zeus was smuggled away by his mother Rhea and hidden in a cave on Crete. After a ten-year struggle Zeus eventually triumphed over Cronos and became ruler of the gods. Zeus' guardians were the Curetes, who prevented his discovery by the clashing of cymbals (see Sappho No.8; Moero No.47).

11: The Daughters of Asopus [22]

'...of your nine daughters, [23] Asopus, three now
are with father Zeus, his to have and hold,
who must rule us all; three more Poseidon,
our Lord of the seas, has taken to wife,
and for two Apollo and one Hermes –

Maia's own true boy [24] – are now the masters
of their beds. Eros and Aphrodite,
the forces of desire, incited them
to enter your house like thieves in the night,
and take their possession of your daughters.

But forever fruitful, forever young,
your girls shall soon rear a stock of heroes,
sons half-mortal, half-divine: this, I swear,
I've seen in the smoke, spoken in the sweat
of lord Apollo's holy oracle.

Such is the mastery of my calling –
for I, Acraephen, [25] alone of fifty
masterful brothers, am prophet supreme
of the most sacred hidden mysteries,
have now seized my own share of divine truth.

---

[22] **The Daughters of Asopus**: As the text of this poem is fragmentary, I
have followed Campbell's supplements (1992: 28ff); Asopus was the name
both of a river in Boeotia and its god.

[23] **nine daughters**: One of Asopus' daughters was Tanagra, who gave her
name to Corinna's city.

[24] **Maia**: Daughter of Atlas and one of the seven Pleiades, she was the
mother of Hermes by Zeus. Hermes rates especial mention here as Tanagra
was a centre for his cult.

[25] **Acraephen**: A mythological prophet, one of Orion's 'high-and-mighty-
sons' (see No.9).

Listen: in the beginning Leto's lad,[26]
Zeus' son, granted the gift of prophecy
to Euonymus,[27] who held this mountain-
shrine until Hyrieus[28] threw him from the land –
became next in line to keep its secrets.

Then Poseidon's son and my own father,
Orion, regained this earth and settled on
this land; today, the hunter once again,
he whirls round and round the darkening skies
and his great prize has fallen to my lot.[29]

And so I learned my chosen trade; to speak
the certainty of faith. And now you too,
friend Asopus, must submit to the will
of heaven: let your mind lie fallow from
its scything grief – father-in-law of gods.'[30]

These were the words of the prophet. At once
Asopus seized his held hand in welcome,
and the tears rolled from his eyes, down and down,
as he began to speak...

---

[26] **Leto's lad**: Apollo, son of Leto by Zeus, and the god of prophecy.

[27] **Euonymus**: Son of Cephisus, a Boeotian river-god, also a prophet.

[28] **Hyrieus**: Son of Poseidon and Alcyone, he entertained Zeus, Poseidon and Hermes when they were travelling through Boeotia disguised as mortals. In return, the three gods provided him with a child, the giant Orion.

[29] Acraephen's genealogy here has been seen as a pointless diversion (Lisi, 1933: 122), or a means to highlight his pomposity and self-absorption (Rayor, 1993: 228). However, Snyder suggests (1984: 131), it is central to the poem's theme of continuity – time past, present and future.

[30] **father-in-law to the gods**: Here Corinna coins a verb *hekoureuein*, 'to be a father-in-law'.

12: Orestes [31]

As the dawn rises [32] from her ocean springs,
she draws the moon's sacred light from the sky;
so, by Zeus' will, seasons slowly change,
winter turning to the flowers of spring;
and now our choir finds pleasure in its pains,
the hard, hard labour of the dance, out through
the seven-gated city [33] [to sing of
Lord Orestes...]

13: Iolaus [34]

[let us worship at the shrine]
        you and I both
                – the two of us
[to make our long-binding vows]

---

[31] **Orestes**: The title given the poem on its manuscript. Orestes has no known connection with Boeotia, but Campbell suggests this poem might have been composed for a girls' choir to perform at the Daphnephoria, a Theban festival of Apollo (1992: 59), since the god had sheltered Orestes after he murdered his mother, Clytemnestra. The attribution to Corinna has been questioned (*PMG* 1962), although a recent study by West (1977: 278ff) argues in favour of her authorship. The text is very fragmentary and here I have followed West's supplements.

[32] **rises**: The Greek here, *liposa*, means simply 'leaving'. Page (1953: 28) reads this as nightfall, i.e. the Dawn leaving the sky. The text is very fragmentary but seems to suggests it is the Ocean which is left behind, as the sun rises above the sea at first light. The rest of the text, if heavily emended, seems to confirm this, particularly the image of spring superseding winter.

[33] **the seven-gated city**: Thebes.

[34] **Iolaus**: According to the commentator who quotes this tiny fragment, the title of the poem from which it is taken. Plutarch records that Iolaus, a mythological hero, had a shrine in Boeotia where lovers used to swear their fidelity – a story which provided my interpretation here (see Introduction p.14).

14: The Muses [35]

I

clear-voiced [Muses
            come] to me

                *

II [36]

leave your sheltered glades
            with honey in your voice
across Euripus' surging straits [37]
            from Olympus
            to meet me here

15:

[Corinna said:]
Athena taught Apollo [38]
                    to play the pipes;
[to hear the music]

16:

from the Muses
            war begins

---

[35] **The Muses**: Often evoked in Sappho's poetry, the Muses have a particular relevance to Corinna's work, through their association with the local mountains of Helicon & Cithaeron (see No.10).

[36] A very fragmentary piece, from a second century AD papyrus, which Campbell suggests is a summons to the Muses (1992: 65).

[37] **Euripus**: The narrow strait separating the island of Euboea from Boeotia, known for its irregular flux, cited proverbially as an indication of fickleness.

[38] **Athena...Apollo**: Traditionally, Apollo was the god of music, usually associated with the lyre. Here Corinna, according to a quotation from Plutarch (*On Music*, 14.1136b), attributes musical invention to Athena, the goddess of wisdom and craft – a statement perhaps about the status of women's poetry?

17: Myrtis [39]

Myrtis is to blame
                    Myrtis, I say –
    swallow-voiced
                    sister-singer –
she strayed into Pindar's strife-torn songs [40]

18: Pindar

As for you, Pindar,
you spoke the Greek
            of city and state:
the language of the market-place [41]

---

[39] **Myrtis**: A woman poet, from Anthedon in Boeotia. An ancient encyclo-paedia claims both Pindar and Corinna were her pupils (*Suda* K 2087). None of her poetry has survived but Plutarch paraphrases her mythological poem on the tragic love of Ochna for Eunostus, a story located, like many of Corinna's, in Boeotia (*Greek Questions*, 40).

[40] The meaning of this fragment has been variously interpreted, with theories resting on the translation of the Greek word *eris* or 'strife'. Traditionally this has been taken here to mean a 'contest', with Corinna chastising Myrtis for com-peting against Pindar (although if the tradition that Corinna defeated Pindar in a poetry competition is to be believed [see below p.34], this might appear contradictory). Snyder suggests it refers to some personal or literary 'quarrel' of which Corinna disapproves (1989: 53). Other studies have seen a struggle between gender-defined poetry, with Myrtis criticised for abandoning local 'women's poetry' in favour of Pindar's 'male' genres (Demand, 1982: 105). I took this hint but added a sense of the theme of such 'male' poetry – often also *eris*, Homer's word for battle.

[41] **market-place**: This fragment is based on a quotation from a scholiast on Aristophanes (*Acharnians*, 720) who comments that Corinna censored Pindar for writing like an Athenian (i.e. using Attic or "pure" Greek rather than their native Boeotian) when he used the verb *agorazein*, 'to spend time in the *agora* or market-place', in one of his poems: in Athens the *agora* was a centre for political as well as commercial life – both exclusively male concerns.

[42] **Metioche and Menippe**: The sisters saved Boeotia from plague after an oracle had decreed that two of Zeus' children had to be sacrificed to purify the city (Zeus was in fact their grandfather by proxy). They were saved by Persephone and Hades, the gods of the Underworld, who turned them into comets. The story also appears in Ovid (*Metamorphoses* 13, 681ff).

19: Corinna's Art

But I sang the glory of local heroes
               hurrahed in our heroines:

20:

[of] Metioche and Menippe [42]
[great Orion's fearless daughters
               shooting stars across the skies]

21:

[or of Antiope] of Hyria [43]
            daughter of this earth
a land fit for dances [44]

22:

[and of you, mother Tanagra,
how] Hermes and Ares
           once came to blows
over you... [45]

---

[43] **Antiope of Hyria**: Daughter of Nycteus, king of Thebes, and mother by Zeus of Amphion. Hyria was a region, and town, in Boeotia.

[44] **land fit for dances**: The literal meaning of the Greek adjective *kallichoros* is 'of beautiful dances (or dancing grounds)'. In the *Odyssey*, Homer uses it extensively as an epithet for cities; here I have read the word as a reference to the women's choruses who sung (and danced) Corinna's songs – with a sly glance back at its heroic antecedent (see Nossis No.83).

[45] Nothing is known of this myth, although Page notes that Hermes was worshipped at Tanagra, and Ares, the god of War, at neighbouring Thebes, suggesting a local rivalry or war behind the legend (Page 1953: 37). I have taken Campbell's suggestion that the fragment refers to the nymph Tanagra (1992: 45).

23:

[And I remembered]
        the fate of Minyas' daughters[46]

24:

[and Hyrie's tears]
for the son she so longed
        to take up in her arms[47]

25: Fragments[48]

And I spoke...
                *
        of myself...
                *
[and for all] of us...
                *
        of our houses...
                *
[of] chine-meat...
                *
                ...and chairs...

---

[46] **Minyas' daughters**: Minyas, a legendary king of Boeotia, had three
daughters who, like Pentheus in Euripides' play the *Bacchae*, were punished
for their refusal to worship Dionysus. In a Bacchic trance they tore their son
and nephew, Hippasos, to pieces, and were then turned into bats. Their story
also appears in Ovid *Metamorphoses* 4.

[47] Apollonius Dyscolus, the grammarian who quotes this fragment, says it
comes from a poem titled 'The Daughters of Euonymus', about whom noth-
ing is known (*Pronouns* 136b). Here I have suggested Hyrie, a mythological
heroine of Boeotia, as a possible subject; when her son Cycnus died, she wept
so much that she was turned into a fountain.

[48] This consists of four tiny quotations, stitched together to create one
poem (see Introduction p.20).

26:

so let us hear this
>   from you

27:

>   for this is your lot:
[the Muses' spoils]

28: At Eros' Shrine

Thespeia, Thespia,[49]
>   your daughters are fair
your lovers, strangers
>   and your strangers, loved;
the Muses hold you in their hearts

29: The Ladon [50]

[roaring river]
>   reed-rearer

---

[49] **Thespeia, Thespia**: The anonymous grammarian who quotes this frag-
ment notes that Corinna has spelt the more usual 'Thespeia' as 'Thespia',
which was at the foot of Mt Helicon, hence its association with the Muses. As
Page notes (1953: 38) it was also celebrated for its cult of Eros, which pro-
vided the title here (see Introduction p.21).

[50] **Ladon**: A river near Thebes, also called Ismenus after a son of Apollo and
Melia. In the text, quoted by the grammarian Theodosius as an example of
proper noun declension, its Greek form *Iadontos* is followed by an internally
rhyming compound adjective in agreement, *donakotropho*, 'a wet nurse for reeds'.
In order to retain some sort of linguistic parallel in English, I made 'Ladon' the
poem's title and supplemented an alliterative first line (see Introduction pp.18-19).

30: Orion of Tanagra

I *The Journey Out*[51]

devout hero
                beast-slayer
land-clearer
                far-traveller
[Tanagra's own]

II *The Voyage Home*[52]

[on the way, take heart:]
no man of envy
                can master you now

                *

But he conquered all
and named the land,
Orion the strong
                for himself...[53]

---

[51] **Orion**: This poem is taken from three separate fragments, all concerned with the legend of Orion. The first section is based on a short paraphrase by a scholiast of a longer work by Corinna. Orion's attributes here are based on his legendary exploits: 'beast-slayer' because he cleared Chios of wild beasts in return for the hand of Merope, daughter of its king, Oenopion; before the wedding, Oenopion, presumably 'the man of envy' of (II), put Orion's eyes out but his sight was restored by travelling eastwards into the sun, hence 'far-traveller'. Orion also features in Adrienne Rich's poem of the same name (1984: 77).

[52] **The Voyage Home**: According to Apollonius Dyscolus, who quotes this fragment (*Pronouns* 105b), the title of the poem from which it comes, although, as Page notes, Orion was known for his ability to walk, rather than sail, on water (1953: 36). Corinna's version of the myth, in which Orion returns from the east to claim his homeland before his death and elevation to the skies, is not known elsewhere.

[53] This fragment, according to Apollonius Dyscolus (98bc), also comes from 'The Voyage Home'. Again, the version of the myth is unique to Corinna (see Page 1953: 36).

31: Boeotus [54]

I

grandson of Cronus

                    Poseidon's sacred boy

it's you, lord Boeotus

II

father of Ogygus [55]

            who forged the gates of Thebes [56]

32: Seven Against Thebes [57]

[after the battle]

            they carried you out

                    [for burial]

---

[54] **Boeotus**: The founding hero of Boeotia, and the son of Poseidon and Melanippe. He was exposed in the woods by his mother, but saved and reared by a shepherd to reclaim his true inheritance later – as is so often the case.

[55] **Ogygus**: A legendary king of Boeotia, which was sometimes known as Ogygia after him. As the scholiast who quotes this fragment points out, Corinna makes him the son of Boeotus, although the more usual legend is that he was fathered by Poseidon.

[56] **gates of Thebes**: one of which was known as 'Ogygia' (see No.12, note 33).

[57] **Seven Against Thebes**: Apollonius Dyscolus, who quotes the fragment, says it derives from a poem of this title (*Pronouns* 119b). The myth concerns Eteocles and Polyneices, the sons of Oedipus and Jocasta; after their parents' death, the two inherited the kingdom of Thebes, each to rule for alternate years. After Eteocles' first year, he refused to hand over power to Polyneices who then gathered a force of seven heroes – one to attack each gate of the city. After ferocious bloodshed, the brothers decided to settle the dispute by single combat, each one dying at the other's hands. The myth was the subject of a play by the fifth-century tragedian, Aeschylus, also called *Seven Against Thebes*. Corinna's use of the verb *komizein*, generally 'to provide or bring' but also with the meaning of 'to carry off for burial', suggested my supplements here.

33: Zeus [58]

[the god] thunders

*

      [calling] to his side

*

the boy with the face of shining glass

34: The Dream

[In my dream, you said:]
Are you still sleeping?
         This isn't you, Corinna
[to drift away the days...] [59]

---

[58] This poem consists of three tiny fragments: the first suggested its title, 'Zeus', as thunder is a common attribute of the god; the second two I placed together as an evocation of the story of Ganymede, the boy Zeus once loved, after one scholar's reading of the third line, although its text is corrupt (Bergk, quoted by Campbell, 1992: 57).

[59] This fragment could derive from a poem in which Corinna is visited by a goddess, possibly in a dream, as my title suggests. Such visitations occur elsewhere in classical women's poetry, most notably in Sappho (LP 1 / Balmer No.78, and possibly in LP 63, a damaged papyrus fragment). Dreams also appear in women's poetry throughout the ages, in artists as varied as Elizabeth Barrett Browning (Bernikow, 1979: p.108) and Anna Akhmatova (McKane, 1989, p.75; 102). Corinna's use of her own name is echoed in other classical women poets, such as Nossis (Nos.72, 79 & 83), Sulpicia (No.88), Julia Balbilla (Nos.95 & 97) and Proba (No.98): see Introduction p.12.

TELESILLA

Telesilla wrote in the Greek city of Argos in the early-fifth century BC. But although Antipater of Thessalonica celebrates her 'wide-ranging fame',[1] little is known of her life and only a handful of her fragments survive, all in quotation, with only one of these any longer than a single word in Greek. Plutarch claims she was a member of a distinguished aristocratic family, and with Pausanias records a story of her courage during an attack on Argos by Cleomenes of Sparta in 494 BC; Telesilla rallied the other women to defend the city, for which she was rewarded with a civic honours, including a public statue.[2]

This story is likely to be apocryphal, invented to explain an annual festival at Argos where men and women exchanged clothes.[3] But Pausanias records that Telesilla won even more honour for her verse than for her valour. He also suggests that her work was written for a female audience, in particular, noting how she was 'highly esteemed by women'.

The paucity of Telesilla'a extant work makes such judgements difficult to assess. Certainly the fragments here seem to suggest that Telesilla's poetry, like that of Corinna, was concerned with local legends, as well as with traditional women's deities, such as Artemis, goddess of both chastity and childbirth, and a regular subject for classical women poets.[4] The mention of a threshing-floor in No.35, also hints at a female environment, as women often sang as they worked (in Plutarch's *Seven Sages*, Thales remarks how he often heard his hostess singing at her hand-mill).[5] However, another commentator states that Telesilla's poems 'roused the Argives', suggesting that she wrote heroic poetry for recitation on public occasions,[6] although no such work is now extant (the early modern poet H.D. was inspired by the image of a warrior-

---

[1] *A.P.* 9.26.5.

[2] Plutarch, *Fine Deeds of Women*, 4.245c-f; Pausanias, *Description of Greece*, 2.20.8-10. Pausanias describes Telesilla's statue, with her poetry books thrown down at her feet and a helmet instead in her hands. Tatian, *Against the Greeks*, 33, also mentions a first-century BC statue of Telesilla by Niceratus.

[3] See Snyder, 1989: 167; Mary Lefkowitz's *The Lives of the Greek Poets* (1981) examines such biographical traditions in more detail.

[4] See Sappho No.8; Nossis No.82.

[5] *Seven Sages*, 14. See No.115.

[6] Maximus of Tyre, *Orations*, 37.5.

lover for her poem 'Telesila' [sic]).[7] What does survive is the high
regard in which Telesilla's poetry was held in antiquity, her poems
valued for their technical innovation and narrative detail.[8]

---

[7] H.D., *Collected Poems*, 1925, pp.272-75.

[8] See No.35, note 11 & No.37, note 17.

[9] **Artemis**: This poem is constructed from three small fragments. Pausanias
(*Description of Greece*, 6.22.9) records how Artemis was pursued by the river-
god, Alpheus; in the more familiar version of the story, found in Ovid's *Meta-
morphoses* 5, the nymph Arethusa is the object of his attentions, and escapes
after being transformed into a fountain by Artemis.

[10] From a comment by Athenaeus, that Telesilla called the threshing-floor,
'the round' (*Scholars at Dinner*, 11.567ff). See No.115.

[11] This fragment is quoted by the commentator Hephaestion (*On Metres*
11.2) as an example of the 'Telesillean' metre – a two or possibly three and a
half foot glyconic line, presumably invented by Telesilla and found also in the
poet Pindar, as well as in Athenian drama and folk songs.

[12] **Coryphum**: A mountain at Epidaurus where Artemis was worshipped
as Artemis Coryphaea. This fragment is based on a reference to a now lost
poem of Telesilla's found in Pausanias' entry for Epidaurus in his *Description
of Greece* (2.82.2).

[13] **Apollo**. Like No.35, this poem has also been constructed from three
small fragments. Apollo was especially worshipped at Argos where, according
to Pausanias (*Description of Greece*, 2.35.2), he had three temples.

35: Artemis [9]

on the round
           of the threshing-floor [10]

*

[sing now of] Artemis, my daughters,
  slipping
        through Alpheus' watery fingers [11]

*

of her mountain temple
           on the peaks of Coryphum [12]

36: Apollo [13]

[and let us sing now of Apollo]
           a song to shine beside the sun [14]

*

        [of his]
      close-curled hair [15]

*

and his son Pythaeus
          who came long ago to Argos
first city of all Greece [16]

---

[14] Athenaeus' quotation, from which this line derives, records that Telesilla called songs to Apollo 'sun-loving' (*Scholars at Dinner*, 14.619b) – he was often characterised as the sun-god, driving his golden chariot across the sky.

[15] **close-curled hair**: The context of this one-word fragment is not known but I have included it here as it seems likely to derive from a description of Apollo, usually depicted with curly hair.

[16] Like Corinna, Telesilla offers local variants of Greek legends, here to praise the worth of her own city, Argos. Like No.35(c), this poem derives from Pausanias' *Description of Greece* (2.35.2).

37: Wisdom

I

[The poet said:]¹⁷
'Women know better:
even how Zeus seduced Hera.' ¹⁸

                    *

II
[The poetess adds:
not only]
            better
[but best]

---

¹⁷ This fragment comes from a scholiast on Theocritus, *Idylls*, 15.64, who comments that, in using the phrase, 'women know best', Theocritus' comic protagonist Praxinoa is 'marvelling at the poet Telesilla', who presumably wrote a poem on the myth of Zeus and Hera (see note 18 below). Here I have incorporated this secondary context into the poem itself, so that it becomes a comment by both Telesilla and Theocritus, 'the poet', on women's wisdom – both mocking and celebratory (see Corinna No.18, note 41; Praxilla No.41, note 12). Section II derives from a one-word quotation in an ancient lexicographer (Hesychius B500) to illustrate a form of the comparative adjective, *beltion* or 'better', used by Telesilla, which Campbell suggests might be feminine plural – 'the better woman' (1992: 81). In carrying over the sense from one section to another here, I have changed the Grrek adjective to an English adverb.

¹⁸ **Zeus and Hera**: This story is recounted by Homer in the *Iliad*, 14.295ff, where already long-married and engaged in bitter squabbling, Zeus is suddenly overcome with desire for his wife, eventually managing to persuade her to rekindle their passion. In common tradition, the intimate details of his seduction were never fully publicised, and so became a by-word for salacious gossip (see Holden, 1974: 210).

PRAXILLA

Praxilla lived in Sicyon, on the gulf of Corinth, during the mid-fifth century BC. Like her near contemporary, Telesilla, very little of her work has survived – eight fragments in all, quoted in ancient commentators, with three providing only passing reference to her work. Hardly anything is known of her life, although Sicyon was renowned throughout early and classical Greece as a city where artistic life flourished. In the first century AD, Antipater of Thessalonica named her among his earthly Muses,[1] although her reputation as the author of *skolia*, songs for drinking-parties, has led some modern commentators to suggest that she might have been a *hetaira* or courtesan – the only women likely to have been present at such events.[2]

Praxilla's reputation has suffered in other ways. The Christian writer Tatian, writing in the mid second century AD, noted a statue erected to her at Sicyon, but concludes that 'she wrote nothing of worth in her poetry'.[3] Also in the second century AD, the rhetorician Zenobius, quoting a snatch of one of her fragments (No.39), records that Praxilla was infamous for the 'silliness' of her work, and that the expression 'sillier than Praxilla' had become proverbial. This could be seen as a typical response to the work of women artists, if the reputation of other poets such as Telesilla, Corinna and Sappho, had not survived intact, at least throughout antiquity. Rather Zenobius' comments seem to reflect a dying knowledge over the centuries of the specifically female context of Praxilla's fragment, a hymn to the fertility god, Adonis, celebrated by women at the annual festival of Adonia.[4] In contrast, the Athenian comic playwright Aristophanes, Praxilla's younger contemporary, borrows from her works for comic effect, assuming a familiarity with and affection for her poetry on the part of his audience.[5]

If occasionally hostile, the sources still reveal the versatility of Praxilla's work, which included not only drinking-songs and hymns but also dithyrambs or choral odes, performed at festivals

---

[1] *A.P.* 9.26.1.3.
[2] See Snyder, 1989: 56.
[3] See Tatian, *Against the Greeks*, 33.
[4] See No.37, note 10.
[5] See Nos.38 & 41.

of Dionysus. Miraculously, examples of each have survived, as well as of the 'Praxilleion', the metre she invented or made famous.[6] Perhaps most interesting of all is the way in which she utilised both 'male' forms and subjects, such as drinking-songs or heroic tales, and 'female', women's festival hymns and the re-telling of local myths, posing questions about how far, even in the deeply segregated society of classical Greece, such art forms were separated.[7]

---

[6] See No.41 (II), note 14.

[7] See Introduction p.11.

[8] This fragment, from a drinking-song, is misquoted by the chorus in Aristophanes' comic play, *Thesmophoriazusae* (528), who change the word 'scorpion' to 'politician' in the playwright's typically satirical style. The original song is attributed to Praxilla by a scholiast on the line – a fitting source for a play set during a women's festival. The lines are also preserved, with slightly different wording and a concluding couplet, as an anonymous drinking-song: it appears that the expression later became proverbial (see No.116).

[9] **Adonis in Hades**: Adonis, a fertility god, was the lover of Aphrodite until killed by a boar. Every year Greek women celebrated the festival of Adonia in his memory, drinking and laughing together and leaving quick-growing vegetables to wither on house-tops for eight days. The exact nature of their festivities still creates a great deal of excitement among scholars (see Detienne, 1977; Winkler, 1990). As Campbell points out (1967: 446), Adonis' words echo Tiresias' question to Odysseus in the *Odyssey* (11.93-94) – why had he forsaken the sunlight for the Underworld?

54

38:

[in love
beware:]
                a scorpion waits
                under every stone[8]

39: Adonis in Hades [9]

The loveliest sight I've left behind is the sun's light
or clear stars on a dark dark sky, a full-faced moon;
and fruits in summer – ripe cucumbers,[10] apples, pears...

40: Achilles [11]

an anger in your heart
                beyond entreaty, beyond hope

---

[10] **cucumbers**: According to the rhetorician Zenobius, it was this comment
which earned Praxilla the repution for stupidity, 'as anyone who sets cucum-
bers beside the sun could only be called ridiculous' (*Proverbs*, 41.21). However,
it seems far more likely to be a reference to the vegetables grown and left to
wither at the Adonia – as Holst-Warhaft has commented, surely 'a misandric
metaphor for the male contribution to fertility' (1992: 100). Whether 'misan-
dric' or not, a cucumber would seem an ideal emblem for any male fertility
god. Praxilla is also punning here on the Greek for cucumber, *sikyos*, and the
name of her city, Sicyon.

[11] **Achilles**: According to Hephaestion, who quotes this fragment, it derives
from a dithyramb, or choral ode about the hero, referring, surely, to his
quarrel with Agamemnon over the Trojan captive, Briseis. This incident opens
Homer's *Iliad*, as Achilles sulks in his tent, refusing to fight, and leads to the
death of Achilles' friend Patroclus, who goes out to battle in his place.

41: Snatches of Song

I [12]

If you want to cheat death like Admetus could,[13]
my friend, let's keep up and keep in with the good.
In the meantime let's drink, let's live and let's learn:
bad company can bring only bad return...

II [14]

Young girl looking out from your high window –
sixteen above but sixty-three below[15]

---

[12] Like No.38, the first two lines of this fragment appear in Aristophanes, who in *The Wasps* (1236) imagines them being sung by some young boyfriend to the politician and general Cleon, a habitual butt of Aristophanes' jokes. The scholiast notes that, although some attribute it to Sappho or Alcaeus, it is in fact one of Praxilla's drinking songs, adding, as proof, another two lines of the verse. Here I have admitted Aristophanes' use of the song alongside Praxilla's authorship, echoing his trademark *double entendre*.

[13] **Admetus**: A mythological king of Pherae in Thessaly. Apollo promised him that he could live forever if someone else would die in his place. When the time came, Admetus asked his parents to oblige but they were less than happy to do so. Eventually his wife Alcestis came forward to sacrifice herself. In Euripides' play, *Alcestis*, the hero Heracles rescues her from the Underworld and returns her to Admetus. Aristophanes' use of these lines in *The Wasps* is particularly apt, as cowardice was one of his favourite gibes at Cleon.

[14] This fragment, again from a drinking-song, is quoted by Hephaestion as an example of the 'Praxilleion', a complicated dactylic metre, apparently invented by Praxilla. The first four words also appear on a vase dated *c*.450 BC.

[15] This line has caused scholars great difficulty. Literally it translates 'with a virgin's head but a wife below' and has usually been interpreted as a reference to loss of innocence, either of a new bride or of a courtesan. One commentator, as Snyder notes, 'finding such a carnal interpretation unbefitting a woman poet' (1989: 57), formulated the theory that it contained a complex metaphor to the moon, inaccessible or 'virginal' high in the sky, but returning to her mythological consort, Endymion, 'a married woman' when she sets below the horizon. I have read the line in the spirit of a party-song, seeing in it an echo of rather more bitter, if witty, anthems to lost loves (see Bob Dylan's *Maggie's Farm* & Introduction p.18, note 56), and translated accordingly.

ERINNA

Erinna lived *c.*350 BC in the region of Rhodes, or possibly on the island of Tenos, and died, according to ancient tradition, at the age of nineteen. Until recently, although highly praised by several ancient commentators, and the subject of several epigrams in the Greek Anthology, her work was known only through three of her own epigrams, memorials to her childhood friend, Baucis, and a few brief quotations from unknown poems; her three-hundred line masterpiece, 'The Distaff' – 'more powerful than those of so many others'[1] – had disappeared without trace. But in 1928, Italian archaeologists unearthed a papyrus which, to great excitement, was found to contain a substantial extract – around fifty-four lines – from the work. To universal surprise, it was discovered that Erinna's poem, like most of her other extant work, and despite the apparently misleading title by which it was known in antiquity, was another lament for Baucis, detailing their childhood memories, the games they played together, and their separation first by Baucis' marriage and then her death.

Since then academic interest in Erinna's work has intensified, with more scholarship devoted to her poetry than that of any other classical women poet, except for Sappho. However, as Donald Levin noted in 1962, fundamental questions about her life and work still remain unanswered: exactly where and when she lived, the nature, even the title of her work, with one scholar even questioning her very existence.[2]

More recent studies by feminist classical scholars have concentrated on the evidence of the text itself, uncovering a sophisticated and complex patterning to Erinna's seemingly random childhood memories. Marilyn Arthur, in particular, has examined the symbolism of the Tortoise game played by the girls in 'The Distaff'.[3]

---

[1] Asclepiades, *A.P.* 7.11.

[2] Levin, 1962: 194-95; West (1977: 116-18) questions whether a girl ('this querulous Cinderella') from an island backwater who spent her days at the loom could really have produced such an accomplished work. He posits instead a brilliant literary 'hoax' written in a women's persona by a male author (see Sulpicia Nos.91 & 92 & p.95). Sarah Pomeroy has leapt to Erinna's defence, arguing that weaving and cultural activity were not mutually exclusive in women's lives, especially during the expanded opportunities of the fourth/third centuries BC (1978: 20).

[3] Arthur, 1980: 58ff; see No.42, note 16 & Anon No.117.

In mythology, she notes, the tortoise was once a young maiden who scorned Zeus and Hera's wedding-feast to stay at home, for which she was condemned to carry her house on her back; in another, the tortoise persuades the eagle to carry her in flight, but falls to her death.[4] In addition, the tortoise's 'straddling' walk makes her not only a delightful toy for the baby Hermes but was associated by some male lyric poets with wantonness and female sexuality.[5] Such links between childhood, death, marriage, home-making, and sexual promiscuity reoccur throughout the poem – links that resonate in my translation.[6] Sarah Pomeroy has also noted associations between the tortoise and both poetry, through the use of its shell as a lyre, and weaving, where hand-looms closely resemble the lyre.[7] Other studies have shown that the poem's title, often thought to have been wrongly attributed to the work by ancient sources, echoes these themes, pointing to the strong metaphorical associations between weaving and death – the thread of life spun by the Fates – as well as the importance of weaving not only in the poem but in the everyday lives of women in antiquity 'a symbol,' as Arthur notes 'of female domesticity'.[8]

Erinna's emphasis on the inner concerns of women echoes that of Sappho, to whom she was often compared in antiquity. Modern commentators have noticed further similarities, from the 'Sapphic intensity' of Erinna's emotion for Baucis,[9] to the creation of a private world of memory, listing the past pleasures the poet shared with her lost companion.[10] Like Sappho, Erinna also employs (and inverts) Homeric language and themes in her poems,[11] while her use of Sappho's Aeolic dialect appears to be a direct semantic homage to the older poet.[12]

But like Corinna, Erinna also writes in the local Doric dialect, and her poems, with so much of women's art, mix 'high' and 'low' forms – folk motifs with epic poetry, formulaic chants with lyric imagery. Her shorter and fragmentary poems display a dazzling versatility, from puns to intricate metaphor, from the prosaic inscription of a gravestone to the lyrical intensity of grief.

---

[4] Aesop's *Fables*, 126; 352.
[5] *Homeric Hymn to Hermes*, 28; Anacreon 458 PMG.
[6] For example, 'the great shell' of the yard in line 8.
[7] Pomeroy, 1978: 19.
[8] See A & A Cameron, 1969: 287; Arthur, 1980: 63.
[9] See Levin, 1962: 193; Snyder 1989: 171, note 46.

42: The Distaff [13]

...the rising moon...

    ...falling leaves...

        ...waves spinning on a mottled shore...[14]

        ...and those games, Baucis,[15] remember?
twin white horses, four frenzied feet – and one Tortoise
to your hare: 'Caught you,' I cried. 'You're Mrs Tortoise now.' [16]
But when your turn came at last to catch the catcher
you raced on far beyond us, out from the great shell
of our smoke-filled yard...

---

[10] A similar list is offered to Atthis in Sappho LP 94 / Balmer No.32 (for a further discussion of memory and loss in classical women's poetry, see Introduction pp.14-15). Memories of childhood are also used by many modern women poets, for example, Carolyn Forché's 'As Children Together', which, like 'The Distaff', directly addresses a lost friend (Forché, 1983: 43).

[11] See Marilyn Skinner's study of the link between Erinna and Homer (Skinner: 1982), and No.42, note 15 below.

[12] See also No.44, note 28. However, Erinna's aversion to Baucis' marriage is in marked contrast to Sappho's celebratory wedding poems. Other women poets to echo Sappho include Nossis, Melinno and Julia Balbilla.

[13] Of the papyrus' fifty-two lines, only these twenty or so can be translated with any sense of continuity. However, even these are very fragmentary, and have been supplemented, with differing results, by both Bowra and West (1936 & 1977). For the most part, I have followed Bowra, although in the absence of any definite text, critical readings play a large part in determining its 'translation'.

[14] These lines derive from phrases which appear earlier in the manuscript.

[15] **Baucis**: Throughout the poem, Erinna uses her friend's name as a refrain or 'recurring cries of sorrow' (Bowra 1936:163). Skinner has shown that this corresponds with the women's laments found in Homer's *Iliad* (1982: 267), and is still a common feature of women's laments in modern Greek folk literature (see Holst-Warhaft, 1992: 36).

[16] **horses...feet...Mrs Tortoise**: These are all references, as Bowra has identified, to a girls' game, similar to 'What's the time, Mr Wolf?', and likewise accompanied by ritual question and answer. The Greek commentator Pollux records that one girl, the 'Tortoise', sat in the middle of a circle of her companions, weaving a shroud for her dead child. As in 'Mr Wolf', questions and answers ensued, here on the subject of the child's death; at the cue 'he leapt from white horses into the sea', the Tortoise rushed at the other girls and whoever she caught replaced her (see No.117).

                    ...Baucis, these tears are your embers
and my memorial, traces glowing in my heart,
now all that we once shared has turned to ash...
                                   ...as girls
we played weddings with our dolls, brides in our soft beds,[17]
or sometimes I was mother[18] allotting dawn wool
to the women, calling for you to help spin out
the thread...
                    ...and our terror (remember?) of Mormo[19]
the monster – big ears, and tongue, forever flapping,
her frenzy on all fours and changing shapes – a trap
for girls who had lost their way...
                         ...But when you set sail[20]
for a man's bed, Baucis, you let it slip away,
forgot the lessons you had learnt from your 'mother'
in those far-off days – no, never forgot; that thief
Desire stole all memory away...
                              ...My lost friend,
here is my lament: I can't bear that dark death-bed,
can't bring myself to step outside my door; won't look
on your stone face, won't cry or cut my hair for shame...[21]
but Baucis, this crimson grief
                         is tearing me in two...

[17] **dolls...brides**: The dolls were made of wax in the images of girls (Bowra, 1936: 155). Their mention here has added poignancy; before marriage, Greek women offered up their childhood dolls to Artemis, the virgin goddess. The reference to their beds may suggest that Erinna and Baucis shared a sexual as well as emotional intensity (see Snyder, 1989: 171, note 46; Levin, 1962: 193).

[18] **mother**: I have followed Page's suggestion that the mother here is neither Erinna's nor Baucis's, as other scholars dispute, but Erinna taking the part of a mother in a game, with Baucis first playing the household servants and then her daughter. This reading adds to the trauma of Erinna's separation from her 'child'.

[19] **Mormo**: In Greek folklore, a mythic female figure invoked to frighten children (see Theocritus *Idyll* 15.40). Again the memory has an added tension in that Mormo, having lost her own children, attempts to kill and devour others, and was also commonly represented as sexually insatiable (see Introduction p.18). Jacqueline Brown's poem, 'Fairy Tale' evokes a modern Mormo, at once monstrous and sympathetic (1993: 24).

[20] **set sail**: The same form of the verb *bainein*, 'to leave' or 'sail away', used by Sappho of Helen's desertion of Menelaus (No.4) has been conjectured by both Bowra and West for the damaged papyrus here. See Introduction, p.17.

43: The Living and the Dead [22]

From here, our fading echoes reach out in vain for Hades;
but the dead know only silence: darkness corrodes the rest.

44: Funeral Prayer [23]

Solonicus, swift fish, sole guide for sailors towards the sun:
guide her soul [through darkness] now from this stern ship
                                        – my sweet sole mate.

---

[21] **step outside my door...for shame**: The interpretation of these lines
has caused scholars great difficulty. It has been suggested that Erinna was a
priestess of a cult which forbade her to look on the dead (Bowra, 1936: 160).
West suggests that the taboo keeping her from the funeral was her status as a
young woman of child-bearing age (1977: 109). Recently Holst-Warhaft has
examined the fear associated with women's roles as mourner (1992: 100ff); in
classical Athens, for example, the right to mourn was limited to kinswomen
of the deceased (see Plutarch *Moralia* 608a; Lysias, 1-8). Holst-Warhaft also
notes that at Delphi even the lamentations of kinswomen were curtailed by
legislation (1992: 115). Whatever the meaning of these lines, Erinna's psycho-
logy is apt; unable to express her grief through the ritual of a funeral, Erinna's
emotion is first intensified then released through poetic creation (see Intro-
duction p.21). The juxtaposition of domesticity and death is also found in
Eavan Boland's poem 'Woman in Kitchen' (1989: 43).

[22] This fragment, quoted by Stobaeus (4.51.4), has also been associated
with Erinna's laments for Baucis. Bowra (1936: 162) suggests it might come
from a lost section of 'The Distaff' (No.42).

[23] This fragment, quoted by Athenaeus (7.283.D), is an example of a *pro-
pempticon*, a poem written to a relative or friend about to undertake a journey,
a form also used by Sappho (LP 5 / Balmer No.80). Here, the context appears
to be a dead soul's journey to the Underworld, and has been associated with
Erinna's laments for her friend Baucis. The Greek contains a pun on the fish
Pompilos, or escort-fish, which swam alongside ships, and the verbs, *pempein*,
'to send' and *pompeuein* 'to escort'. In English I have used another pun, sole/
soul (see Introduction p.19).

61

45: At Baucis' Tomb[24]

I

My name is Baucis, Bride.[25] Be moved to tears as you pass by
my lonely stone, and leave this message for the grasping dead:
'Hades, you sell your souls to envy.' Then look on these words
and despair at Baucis' savage fate – how once she was married
but with those wedding torches her funeral pyre was lit.[26]
And now you, Lord Hymen,[27] have slowed her solemn wedding march
to that weeping winding crawl towards the wide, waiting grave.

*

II [28]

Let my slab, two stone sirens, and much-lamented urn –
their sparse grey ashes turned Hades' subjects now – cry Hail
and then Farewell to those who pass by my cold dark tomb –
be they city friends or strangers from some other state.
Tell them these bricks entomb a bride, and say this also;
that my father once named me Baucis, that I was raised
at Tenos,[29] if they want to know, and that my soul-mate
Erinna branded this lonely grave with my short life.

---

[24] These two epigrams were preserved, with No.46, in the Greek Anthology (*A.P.*7.712 & 710). Another inscriptional poem by a woman to a dead friend is Anne King's seventeeth-century tribute to Dorothy, Lady Hubert (Greer, 1988: 182).

[25] The association of death with marriage is also found in modern Greek folksongs, for example: 'Just tell them that I have taken the tombstone as my mother-in-law, the black earth as wife...' (quoted and translated by Holst-Warhaft, 1992: 181).

[26] **wedding torches...funeral pyre**: In Kostis Palamas' 1960 poem *Thanatos Pallikariou* ('Death of a Brave Lad'), a mother laments her son, asking mourners to 'light candles for him and yellow funeral pyres / to light the fair young man as he descends to Hades' (quoted and translated by Holst-Warhaft, 1992: 177).

[27] **Hymen**: The god of marriage.

[28] I have followed Giangrande's text and reading here (Giangrande: 1969).

[29] **Tenos**: An island in the Cyclades, in the Aegean sea. According to some sources, it was also Erinna's home.

46: Portrait of Agatharchis [30]

With skill and love these delicate lines were drawn –
                                        Prometheus [31]
take care: we on earth can still command your skill;
this portrait has her so very true to life;
add a voice and Agatharchis is complete –
                                        both smiles and speaks.

---

[30] Like Nos. 42 & 43, preserved in the Greek Anthology (*A.P.*6.352).

[31] **Prometheus**: A legendary Titan, who, in one myth, created mankind by fashioning it out of clay.

MOERO

Moero is believed to have lived around 300 BC in the then Greek city of Byzantium. An ancient source records that she was the wife of one Andromachus, who may have been the author of an etymological dictionary, and the mother of Homerus, a tragic poet.[1] She is known to have written hexameter verse, hymns, lyrical and elegiac poetry, although only two epigrams survive in the Greek Anthology,[2] as well as a ten-line extract from what appears to be an epic poem on the mythology of the Greek god Zeus.

Although she was honoured with a statue in antiquity, and the male epigrammatist Meleager referred to her poems as 'lilies',[3] even those modern scholars sympathetic to classical women's poetry find it difficult to praise her work. Her epigrams have been described as 'affected', while her hexameter poem on Zeus has been seen as 'commonplace' and 'of no great originality'.[4] Such judgements seem rather hasty. True, Moero's epigrams might appear stilted in comparison with Anyte's more playful, approachable poems, or Nossis' sensualism, but they are not without skill; No.48, for example, sets up a neat, almost poignant, opposition between the picked grapes and its lost mother-branch – between the goddess of love's shrine, and the sensualism of the tendril still curled around the vine.[5]

Likewise, her epic account of Zeus' childhood represents a learned homage to Homer's epic, as one might expect from the member of such a scholarly family. But while she echoes the heroic epithets of the *Iliad* and the *Odyssey*, her verse also features some teasing word-play and internal rhyme (*aietos aiev; trerones...traphon... trerosi*), all of which I have rendered here by a similarly 'archaic' but playful alliterative verse.[6]

---

[1] *Suda:* entry on 'Myro'.

[2] *A.P.*6.119; *A.P.*6.189.

[3] Tatian, *Against the Greeks*, 32; *A.P.*4.1.5.

[4] Snyder 1989: 85; Gow & Page 2. 414; Snyder 1989: 86.

[5] For a modern equivalent, see Jo Shapcott's 'Vegetable Love' (1993: 14).

[6] See Thom Gunn's version of Ovid, 'Arethusa Saved' (Hofmann & Lasdun, 1994: 143-44).

47: The Childhood of Zeus [7]

Lord Zeus was once fostered in Crete
        far from the blessed gods
safe from his father's searing sight.
           And his strength slowly grew.
Deep in a timeless cave he dwelt
        tended by trembling doves
and suckled on sweet ambrosia
        from soft ocean streams;
a great eagle
      always eager
        gnawed nectar from a rock
for the bird to bear in his beak
        a beaker for wise Zeus.
Triumphing over father Cronos
        far-thundering Zeus
made the eagle an immortal
        his intimate on high. [8]
And those timorous trembling doves
        he treasured too above
set them in heaven's skies
        our seasons' timeless harbingers. [9]

---

[7] **The childhood of Zeus**: For the background to this myth see No.10, note 21 (see also Sappho No.8).

[8] **eagle...intimate on high**: This myth explains why the eagle became Zeus' emblem.

[9] **our seasons' timeless harbingers**: In one version, doves (*peleiai*) were associated with the constellation of the Pleiades, due to the similarities between their Greek names. More usually, the Pleiades were characterised as seven sisters, pursued by the hunter Orion, and set like him in the sky. Their rising marks the beginning of summer, and their setting, the beginning of winter. For Orion, see Nos.11, 19, 20 & 30.

48: A Temple Offering [10]

Hang there, beneath Aphrodite's golden pillars,
temple grapes, heavy with the wine-god's heady sap;
your mother-vine is curled around her lover branch,
won't hold your head again between her scented leaves.

49: Cleomenes' Statues

Forest nymphs, immortal daughters of woodland streams,
                                        dark, divine,
whose wild-rose feet tread down and down the tangled depths,
Cleomenes sends you Greetings: preserve his health
who preserves your sacred beauty by these statues
                                        carved from pine.

---

[10] The epigram describes either a real bunch of grapes dedicated at Aphrodite's temple, or a dedicatory drawing of grapes.

ANYTE

Like Moero and Erinna, Anyte flourished around 300 BC, and, according to one ancient source, lived in the Arcadian city of Tegea in the Greek Peloponnese.[1] Twenty-one of her poems survive, all epigrams, an artificial genre much loved of Hellenistic poets which owed its genesis to the real inscriptions – both sepulchral and dedicatory – carved in stone throughout antiquity. By the third century BC, this had become the model for sophisticated literary exercises intended primarily for publication. Anyte's subjects include the traditional laments for the dead, particularly of mothers for their daughters, and temple offerings, as well as more innovative pastoral scenes, animal poetry and memorials for dead pets.

Such apparently whimsical concerns have upset male scholars and feminist revisionists alike. Gilbert Highet's truncated entry in the *Oxford Classical Dictionary* manages a double-edged 'charming', although F.A. Wright praises her work as 'masculine'.[2] He finds a surprising ally in the feminist scholar Marilyn Skinner, who complains, as of Corinna, that in her laments for fallen warriors – and their horses – Anyte 'follows the dominant literary tradition.'[3] By contrast, the ostensibly sympathetic Sylvia Barnard sees the poet primarily as 'a wife and mother,' declaring that 'nothing in her poetry indicates that she would not have accepted that role'.[4]

Patriarchal lackey or purveyor of domestic whimsy? Interestingly, Anyte's art lies in her ability to straddle the two. As a recent study has shown,[5] her work is packed with knowing references to Greek literary culture, particularly the epic poems of Homer, but also to archaic lyric, Attic drama, and even a treatise by Xenophon on horse-rearing.[6] And where poets such as Sappho and Erinna subvert such traditions to create a parallel women's world within their work, throughout her poetry, Anyte teasingly deflates heroic conventions – until a yapping puppy is characterised as a Homeric warrior, or a babbling brook, an epic roaring ocean.[7]

---

[1] Pollux, 5.48.
[2] Wright, 1923: 328.
[3] Skinner, 1991: 43, note 29.
[4] Barnard, 1978: 210.
[5] Geoghegan: 1979.
[6] See No.60, note 34.
[7] See No.61, note 36; No.57, note 29; Introduction p.14.

Anyte's own poetics, too, are stunning. Her epigrams brim with playful tropes and devices, witness the onomatopoeic alliteration of 's' in her paean to a cicada, or the repeated barking 'k' of her elegy for a puppy.[8] Or the use of both internal and end rhymes to create a sense of pathos in her moving lament for Thersis, and the coining of witty compound adjectives.[9]

But the most important of Anyte's innovations are those for which she has been most derided: her pastoral poems and pets' epitaphs, both genres which later became standard for any self-respecting Hellenistic epigrammist. In particular, Anyte's poems for pets were widely copied, with Marcus Argent producing an imitation of No.63, and Ovid of No.60,[10] while the Greek Anthology contains several epigrams with striking similarities to Anyte's work.[11] In addition, her vivid depiction of pastoral scenes – a cooling spring or fertile mountain slopes – is now believed to have greatly influenced the male poet Theocritus, often seen as the founding-father of pastoral poetry.[12] It hardly seems coincidental, as Jane Snyder notes, that Anyte was associated by the ancients with Arcadia, the region characterised in later poetry as an idyllic pastoral paradise, or that her poetry contains several references to the archetypal Arcadian deity, Pan.[13]

Anyte's pastoral poems reveal another aspect of her art: her economy. No.58, for example, uses the sensual sea landscape to intertwine Aphrodite's dual characterisation as both an ocean and love goddess.[14] Similarly in her lament for a beached dolphin, sea, ship and beast are mutually associated through verbs of rising and falling.[15]

Despite their seemingly trite or domestic settings, these poems, like all of Anyte's work, reveal a razor-sharp wit, scholarly learning and above all, technical excellence.[16] And if her 'celebrations

---

[8] Nos.51 & 61.

[9] No.50; see No.70, note 60.

[10] *A.P.*7.364; *Metamorphoses*, 10.121ff.

[11] See *A.P.*7.200 (Nicias) which corresponds to No.62; *A.P.*7.212 (Mnasalces) which echoes No.65.

[12] See Luck, 1954: 181, although Tarn (1961: 276) considers Theocritus the sole originator of the genre.

[13] Snyder, 1989: 67, see Nos.56 & 70.

[14] Similarly, in Sappho LP 2 / Balmer No.79, the sensual qualities of Aphrodite and her sacred grove are interwoven (see No.58, note 30).

[15] See No.64.

[16] Her nearest modern equivalents might be Stevie Smith or Marianne Moore, whose poems can also appear 'over-whimsical' but are likewise accomplished, learned and extremely influential.

of military prowess' appear to 'idealise warfare',[17] then her epitaphs for daughters by mothers' redress the balance, continuing a tradition of women's poetry from Sappho onwards, and celebrating one of the most powerful female relationships.[18]

---

[17] Skinner, 1991: 30 & 43, note 29.

[18] See Nos.50 & 51; Sappho No.3; Nossis No.78; Anonymous Nos.102-05. For a modern model see Eavan Boland 'The Pomegranate', a re-working of Ovid's tale of Ceres and Persephone (in Hofmann & Lasdun, 1994: 140).

50: I Philainis [19]

Over and over at this small tomb, Cleina weeps in sorrow,
a mother lamenting her daughter,
                                    the final race which death has won.

Again and again she calls to you, her dearest Philainis,
you sailed away but not to marriage [20]
                                    across green-gloaming Acheron. [21]

51: II Thersis

Instead of a beautiful bridal bed and sacred wedding hymns,
your mother now offers up this marble tomb, this statue;
it has your measure,
                    the pleasure in your face,
                                    your virgin treasure –
O Thersis, we can still celebrate you, even in death.

---

[19] **Philainis**: Geoghegan has noted (1979: 68) that this epigram echoes Achilles'
mourning of Patroclus in the *Iliad* (23.218-24), although Homer's analogy is of a
father grieving for his son, more usually the mourner named in sepulchral epi-
grams (see Nos.102, note 9 & 103, note 10). Here a mother is not only chief
mourner for her daughter, but she is also mentioned by name – a rare occurrence.

[20] **sailed away**: Anyte uses the same verb form here (*eba* from *bainein*, 'to
leave' or 'sail away') as Sappho uses of Helen in No.4 and Erinna possibly uses
of Baucis in 'The Distaff' (No.42).

[21] **green-gloaming Acheron**: Acheron was the river of the Underworld,
qualified here by the adjective *chloros*, also used by Sappho (see No.2, note 24).
Again I have translated it as 'green'; however, it was particularly associated in
Greek poetry with moisture or water (see No.53), and has a root meaning of
'shining', related to the Anglo-Saxon *zlom* ('twilight') from which we get
'gloaming' (see Irwin 1974: 32). The addition here of 'gloaming' keeps the
alliteration of Anyte's original.

A Father's Grief

52: I Antibia

This lament is for Antibia, a virgin. Many bridegrooms – [22]
in hope, at least – came to her father's house,
drawn by word of her beauty, and her wisdom's growing fame. [23]
                                                    But Fate,
the destroyer, swept all such hopes away
                                        far from reach.

53: II Erato

These are the last things:
                    throwing her arms around her dear father
Erato spoke, her tears flowing, fresh-water pearls: [24]
'Father, I am fading fast, the darkness falling on my eyes,
and I am slipping into it
                    towards black Death.'

---

[22] **bridegrooms**: Gow & Page complain that the term is 'loosely-used' (1965: 94); Antibia did not live long enough to marry any of her suitors. Geoghegan suggests (1979: 75) that her hopeful lovers saw themselves already married to her – a reading I have included here.

[23] **her beauty and her wisdom's fame**: These words echo Penelope's description of Pandarus' daughters in the *Odyssey* (20.70-1).

[24] **tears...fresh-water pearls**: In the Greek (literally 'with green tears'), Anyte uses the colour term *chloros* (see 'green-gloaming Acheron in No.50), which could mean anything from pale yellow to dark green, but here, perhaps, contrasts the paleness of Erato's tears with the 'darkness' of her death. I also wanted to hint at the gleaming moisture associated with the adjective (see Irwin, 1974: 35ff; No.50, note 21; Sappho No.2, note 24), often used to convey vigour and life – for which pearls, in this context, seemed a poignant metaphor.

Pastorals

54: Cool Spring I

Sit, one and all, under the spreading leaves of this laurel,
drink the sweet water of this season's spring;
if you're gasping for breath in the heat of harvest,

                                                  rest here:
let the West-Wind breeze strike its cooling blows.[25]

55: Cool Spring II

Stranger, rest your aching body beneath these cool rocks
where winds murmur through fresh green leaves:[26]
drink the cool spring water – welcome relief,

                                               brief respite
for travellers in the scorching heat.

---

[25] **strike...its blows**: This metaphor is an echo of Homer's description of the west wind in the *Iliad.* 11.305.

[26] **fresh green leaves**: Again Anyte uses the adjective *chloros*, here to convey the lushness of the spring's surrounding trees (see Nos.50 & 53).

[27] See No.70, note 69.

[28] **fertile ground**: Anyte uses a rare technical term, *eutokos*, which means 'giving birth easily', an interesting choice for a woman poet (see Geoghegan 1979: 168-69).

[29] **murmurs**: In the Greek, Anyte uses a compound of the Homeric verb *iachein*, applied in his epic poems to the roar of the sea. With ironic bathos, she applies it to a more domestic setting, a babbling roadside spring.

[30] **oil-smooth**: The Greek adjective, *liparos* means 'shining', 'anointed' or 'glistening with oil', an appropriate epithet for the goddess's statue – Greek lovers often anointed each other with oil, while Aphrodite anointed the body of her lover Adonis after his death (see Nossis No.78, note 41). Geoghegan points out that the term was also used in Greek poetry of a calm sea (1979: 148). In a single word, Anyte draws together her four themes – the sea, fear of death, love and 'comfort'.

56: A Lonely Piper

'Why do you sit in this dark and lonely grove
                         Pan the herdsmen, Pan the hunter,[27]
picking out your song on such sweet-sounding pipes?'

'So that my calves might graze on these dew-drenched hills
                         – my favoured flock on fertile ground [28]
harvesting their fair crop of its fine-grained corn.'

Statues of the Gods

57: Travellers' Rest

I am Hermes, who stands beneath this row of swaying trees
where three roads meet by a foam-white beach.

I hold out hope of rest for those wearied by their journey;
a spring murmurs here, so cold and clear.[29]

58: Aphrodite by Sea

This place is sacred to the goddess.
                         Here her constant pleasure
is to watch the sea as it shimmers from the shore,
and ensure the comfort of sailors;
                         all around the ocean
trembles as it gazes on her statue, oil-smooth.[30]

59: False Pride

Gaze with wonder on the wine-god's horny goat [31]
                                             – how haughtily [32]
he looks down on us, transfixed by his own shaggy locks;
he's puffed with pride because so often now on soft slopes
                                             some nymphs
have held a curl of that rough hair in their rose-white hands.

60: Children's Games [33]

They've reined you in, Mr Goat, with a crimson bridle,
and a nose-band for your shaggy neck;
the children are training you, [34] a horse for the course,
racing round and round the god's own shrine – [35]
if you can still bear their not-so-tame teasing games.

---

[31] **Gaze on... the wine god's goat**: An epigram on a picture or relief depicting a goat.

[32] **haughtily**: Anyte here humorously employs an epic adverb *agerochos*, used by Homer of proud heroes (see Geoghegan, 1979: 138-39).

[33] **Children's Games**: See Erinna's 'Distaff' (No.42).

[34] **training you**: Anyte uses the verb, *paideuein*, generally 'to bring up children', in its specific sense of training a horse to respond to the bit (see Xenophon, *On Horsemanship*, 10.6) – an ironic reversal with children as trainers, not trained.

[35] **the god's own temple shrine**: Geoghegan points out that the child Dionysus was occasionally portrayed riding a goat (1979: 131).

[36] **you met your fate...**: This is an echo of the opening of Andromache's lament for Hector in the *Iliad* (24.725). The epigram contains many other references to epic poetry, teasingly characterising the puppy as a lost hero.

[37] **swiftest to bark**: Anyte coins an onomatopoeic Greek epithet, *philophthoggos*, which literally means 'noise-loving' (see Geoghegan, 1979: 108). The image (and effect) is echoed by Stevie Smith's barking dog in her poem, 'Heartless' (in Barker, 1988: 25).

61: A Lost Puppy

You met your fate like those great dogs of old [36]
                            by the curling roots
of a coward's bush; Loci, of Locri,
swiftest of pups – especially to bark, [37]
into your light paws he sank harsh poison
                    that speckle-necked snake. [38]

62: Epitaph for a Cicada [39]

Wings whirling, oars rowing into daylight, [40]
they'll rouse me, my friend, from my bed no more:
for as you slept, Robbie the Ravager [41]
crept up on you so stealthily, so quiet,
and with his clumsy nail
                    cut your tiny throat.

---

[38] **speckle-necked snake**: Again Anyte is the only poet to use the compound adjective, *poikilodeiros*, found in the epic poet Hesiod to describe a nightingale, of a snake.

[39] **Epitaph for a Cicada**: The interpretation of this epigram has proved problematic: some commentators, confused by the wake-up calls of line 2, have argued that its subject is a cockerel, rather than a cicada, as ancient sources stated. Geoghegan convincingly argues in favour of the latter, and I have followed his reading here (1979: 112-13). For a modern equivalent, see Marianne Moore's 'To a Snail'.

[40] **oars rowing**: Anyte uses an extraordinary metaphor of the cicada rubbing its wings like oars, employed elsewhere by Aeschylus in *Agamemnon* (52) and Euripides in *Ion* (161) of birds beating their wings in flight. The Greek verb *epessein* means 'to speed by rowing' which I took to include a temporal as well as physical motion.

[41] **Robbie the Ravager**: The Greek *sinis* or 'robber' derives from the legendary villain, Sinis, whose name was used proverbially (see Introduction pp.18-19).

63: Two Lost Friends

The nightingale of the turf and the native of the trees –
for her grasshopper and her cicada
                              Myro [42] fashioned a common grave;
and her tears fell from those virgin cheeks for her two lost toys;
Hades has them now, took them for his own –
                              are forfeit he would never waive. [43]

64: A Dolphin's Farewell

Never again will I find my god in the swimming seas,
my neck rising and falling beneath the depths.
No, I won't blow around the ship's lovely bow, in and out
by smooth oar-holes, a figurehead delighted
into life; [44] for the waves' dark swell has cast me on dry land,
and I lie there now, beached by this soft sea-shore. [45]

---

[42] **Myro**: It has been conjectured that this is a reference to the poet Moero, sometimes spelt Myro. Although it is unlikely that Anyte and Moero were childhood friends as one scholar suggested (see Geoghegan 1979: 173), the use of such a rare name here is interesting (see Nossis, No.77, note 35).

[43] **Hades...waive**: The god of the Underworld is here portrayed as a petulant child, destroying his playmate's pet.

[44] **a figurehead...into life**: Dolphins were often used as figureheads for Greek ships. Jane Snyder has pointed out that this allusion plays with the traditional insistence of epigram on the likeness of a work of art to its subject (Snyder, 1989: 72; see No.51).

[45] **beached by this soft sea shore**: In antiquity, dolphins were thought to cast themselves ashore for burial (see Oppian, *Halieutica*, 2.628ff).

65: The War-horse

A memorial for my horse, battle-hard:[46]
                Damis sees her now
slain when the war-god's shaft pierced her spotted flank;[47]
her dark blood seethed beneath her skin, true shield-guard,[48]
                spattering dark gore
on this earth, seeping through soil we both have ploughed.[49]

Heroes' Graves

66: Amyntor

This hardening Lydian soil holds him now,
                Amyntor, Philip's son,
the harsh iron of battle in his soul.
Yet not plague nor pain destroyed him, drove him
into that darkening Night,[50] but courage,
his round shield arched above his battle-friend.[51]

---

[46] **battle-hard**: The epithet *menedeios*, 'standing one's ground in battle', is used in Homer of warriors; here, Anyte vividly characterises the dead horse as an epic hero.

[47] **spotted**: The Greek adjective *daphoinos* literally means 'blood-red' but is used by Homer of beasts of prey; Anyte's horse is not only a bay but 'spotted' with the blood of battle (see Geoghegan, 1979: 99). It can also mean 'bloody' or 'murderous'.

[48] **shield-guard**: In Homer the epithet *talaurinos* is used of the war-god Ares, and means 'carrying a hide-covered shield'. Here Anyte uses it to describe the horse's skin – both a hide and a shield.

[49] **both have ploughed**: As farmers and farm-horse, and as warrior and war-horse, perhaps?

[50] **Night**: Used as a metaphor for death in Greek poetry from Homer onwards.

[51] **his battle-friend**: This line echoes Homer's description of Ajax protecting Teucer in the *Iliad* (8.269ff).

67: Pheidias [52]

Captain, our Captain, now we have laid you out to rest.
                      O Pheidias,
the youth of your city in the gloom of grief, children lost
without their mother. [53] But listen: the stone above your grave
                      sings your praises, [54]
your fate: how you fell fighting for your fair fatherland.

Offerings

68: I The Battle Spear [55]

Rest now, my slayer spear, relieved at last of battle blood
which falls drop by drop, dark tears, from your bronze claw. [56]
Raise your banner in Athena's towering marble halls; [57]
trumpet the triumphs of Echecratidas
                    from Crete.

---

[52] **Pheidias**: Geoghegan points to the many literary allusions in this epigram – to Homer in line 1, Aeschylus' *Persians* in line 2 and the poets Theognis and Tyrtaeus in lines 3 and 4 (1979: 57).

[53] **mother**: In the *Iliad*, Teucer runs towards Ajax's shield like 'a child to its mother's skirts' (see note 52 above).

[54] **sings your praises**: In contrast to the allusions throughout the poem, this metaphor is Anyte's own.

[55] Geoghegan has noted the 'almost unique' use of imperatives in this epigram, which echo those of the parade ground (1979: 17). This epigram was imitated by the male Hellenistic poets Callimachus and Nicias.

[56] **bronze claw**: The spear's head: Geoghegan suggests that the spear is characterised as a living being standing on its feet (1979: 24).

[57] **Athena's towering marble halls**: Athena's temple was a prominent feature of ancient Tegea.

69: II The Great Bowl

A pot like an ox.[58]
>   Eriaspidos' son put it here,
Cleubotos, who calls wide Tegea fatherland.
A labour for Athena,
>   Aristoteles made it,
of Cleitor,[59] called by his father's broadening name.

70: III A Gift for a God

To Pan the Panicker[60] and his guardian nymphs of stall and spring,
Theudotus, lone shepherd on shady peaks, donated this gift;[61]
for in the scorching scented heat of harvest[62] his suffering
they ceased, held out their hands with cooling water, honey-sweet.[63]

---

[58] **pot like an ox**: The Greek compound adjective, *bouchandes* ('holding an ox'), is almost certainly an invention of Anyte's. Geoghegan notes the association of oxen both with size and value in classical poetry – ox-hides were a common prize for games in Homer – and posits that the bowl was perhaps Cleobotos' own prize for a sporting victory (1979: 31; 33).

[59] **Cleitor**: A town in the north of Arcadia.

[60] **Pan the Panicker**: Pan was thought to be responsible for the fear or 'panic' which caused animals to stampede in remote places. Here Anyte again invents a compound adjective, *phrixokomes*, which literally means 'with hair standing on end' – a reference to the god's hairy appearance. Geoghegan points out that Anyte characterises Pan as both inducing and suffering panic (1979: 43).

[61] **Theudotos…gift**: The name means 'a placed gift', another of Anyte's joking compounds.

[62] **harvest**: Probably of wine.

[63] **honey-sweet**: The Greek adjective, *melichros* is more usually used of wine. Instead, Anyte make a teasing transference; Theudotus harvests the vine but only has water to quench his thirst. The adjective also echoes Sappho No.1 (II) and Nossis No.72.

HEDYLE

Hedyle lived in Athens in the third century BC – the only extant Athenian woman poet, although Athenaeus records that her mother, Moschine, about whom nothing else is known, was also a poet.[1] Only a few lines of her work survive, a fragment quoted by Athenaeus from her mythological poem, *Scylla*.

It is difficult to draw any judgements from such scant evidence, but Hedyle's fragment is nevertheless of great interest to the study of classical women's poetry. Firstly, her choice and treatment of her subject is telling; in Homer's *Odyssey*, written around 700 BC, Scylla is described only as a six-headed monster, snatching sailors from their ships.[2] At the beginning of the first century AD, Ovid focused on Scylla's earlier incarnation as a beautiful young girl who rejected the advances of Glaucus, a merman;[3] Glaucus sought the help of the sorceress Circe (also late of the *Odyssey*) but falling in love with him herself, she jealously transformed Scylla into a monster. Hedyle's fragment, written between the two, is also concerned with the courtship of Scylla by Glaucus. But where Ovid's Glaucus is overcome by sexual passion, wooing Scylla only with an account of his own troubles, Hedyle's is tender and hesitant, furthering his suit with lovers' gifts.[4]

There is artifice, too, in Hedyle's listing of these gifts; as Diane Rayor has pointed out, sea-shells and coral are appropriate presents from a merman to a sea-nymph.[5] Even more interesting is Glaucus' choice of kingfisher-chicks; in antiquity, these were given by lovers as symbols of their undying love, after the myth of Alcyone, who threw herself into the sea when her lover, Ceyx, was drowned. Both were transformed into kingfishers, or *alcyones*. Athenaeus records that in Hedyle's poem the rejected Glaucus, too, drowns himself. But kingfishers had other associations in clas-

---

[1] Athenaeus, *Scholars at Dinner*, 7.297A. But 'anonymous' inscriptions, possibly by women, survive, see Nos.101; 104-06; 109.

[2] *Odyssey*, 12.85ff

[3] *Metamorphoses*, 13.904ff & 14.66ff.

[4] But a fragment from the fifth-century poet Timotheus appears to contain a reference to 'Scylla's gifts' (PMG: No.794). For a modern reworking of Ovid's version, see Vicki Feaver's 'Circe' (Hofmann & Lasdun, 1994: 278-79).

[5] Rayor, 1992: 194. See also pp.58-59 on Erinna's choice of childhood memories in 'The Distaff' (No.42).

sical culture – the Greeks coined the phrase 'halcyon days' after the fourteen calm winter days when the birds built their nests. In *Scylla*, Glaucus hopes for 'calm weather' but his love proves equally short-lived. By a seemingly artless detail, Hedyle weaves a complex and ironic association of faith and betrayal, hope and disappointment, love and grief.

Hedyle's chain of references to monstrous Homeric heroines – not just Scylla, but also the Sirens,[6] and by implication, Circe, is also telling; like so many other classical women poets,[7] she re-reads Homer, distorting his portraits of dangerous women into more sympathetic models.

---

[6] See No.71, note 13.

[7] See Sappho No.4. For modern reinterpretations of these 'monstrous women', see Judith Kazantzis' 'Circe' (1980: 18-19) and Margaret Atwood's 'Circe/Mud Poems' & 'Siren Song' (1976: 201 & 195); see also Introduction p.18.

71: Scylla [8]

'I brought you shells, Scylla,[9] from clear coral reefs [10]
and king-fisher chicks, still learning how to fly –
those halcyon days to come.[11] All these I gave
without faith, without hope.'[12]

At Glaucus' grief
Sirens wept,[13] his fellow dwellers of the deep;
and they swam in sorrow from their rocky shore
by simmering Etna.

---

[8] **Scylla**: According to Athenaeus, the title of Hedyle's poem (7.297A).

[9] **I…Scylla**: The first part of the Athenaeus quotation lacks a main verb, and so, to express Glaucus' intensity of emotion, I used the first person here. Likewise, Scylla is mentioned only as 'the nymph', but is the implied object of Glaucus' attention.

[10] **coral reefs**: In the Greek, 'Erythraean rock'. The Erythraean, or literally Red Sea, was the Indian Ocean off the coast of Arabia, named either because of its red sands or red waters.

[11] **halcyon days to come**: In the text Glaucus' gifts are qualified only as *athurmata*, literally 'trinkets' or 'delights'. I expanded my translation here to emphasise the patterning of kingfisher associations in the text (see pp.80-81).

[12] This line comes from one Greek word in the text, *duspistos*, which can be read as either 'without hope' or 'distrustful'; here, the use of repetition admits both readings.

[13] **Sirens**: In the *Odyssey* (12.167ff), women whose beautiful songs lured unwary men to their deaths. Later, they were often characterised, particularly on Attic vase paintings, as birds of prey with women's faces. Here, as with Scylla, there is no hint of the Sirens' later monstrous incarnations; instead, their songs empathise with Glaucus' distress.

NOSSIS

A contemporary of Anyte's, Nossis also wrote epigrams, of which eleven survive, with a possible twelfth (No.82), also attributed to her. Like so many of the woman poets, she lived on the edge of the Greek world, in the city of Locri in Southern Italy, as she reveals with pride in one of her poems (No.83). Like Sappho, to whom Nossis compared herself,[1] her poetry is concerned with the inner world of women, praising their beauty and spiritual qualities, celebrating the deities of female life, and the emotional relationships between women both within families and in friendship.

Nossis' self-association with the poetry of Sappho, not only through her own declaration but in her many thematic and semantic homages to the older poet's work,[2] has led commentators to suggest that she, too, addressed a circle of women friends, who shared relationships of an erotic intensity.[3] This theory is supported by the attitude of some ancient sources, particularly Hellenistic comic writers, who saw Nossis, like Erinna, as a daughter of Sappho, inventing ribald tales about all three.[4] While such tales were a mainstay of ancient comedy, reflecting, perhaps, more an unease about the status of women writers, than any real concern for their sexual, preferences,[5] Nossis' work certainly presents a uniquely female perspective. Her series of poems celebrating the beauty of prostitutes, for example, emphasise their 'glory' in explicitly heroic language,[6] as well as the moral virtue of their lives.[7] Such poems make an interesting comparison with those by male poets, such as Leonidas or Julianus, which portray their courtesans as grasping and vain, concentrating on the wealth of their temple-offerings rather than Nossis' insistence on the spiritual qualities of the donors.[8]

---

[1] See No.83.

[2] See Nos.72, 77, 78, 82 & 83.

[3] See Skinner, 1991: 21; 34-35. For a discussion of Nossis' linguistic and thematic debt to Sappho, see Skinner, 1989.

[4] Including joint shopping expeditions for leather dildoes (see Herodas, *Mimes*, 6).

[5] See Lefkowitz, 1981a: 59-68 for a discussion of the portrayal of women writers as 'sexual deviants' throughout the ages & Balmer, 1992: 7-8.

[6] See No.73, notes 24 & 25.

[7] See No.74, note 27 & No.76, note 34.

[8] *A.P.* 6.211, translated in Jay, 1981: 99; *A.P.* 6.19 & Jay, 1981: 311; see also Alexis, fragment 15. For a further discussion of the differences between Nossis and the male epigrammatists, see Arthur, 1977: 78.

Some scholars believe that such gynocentricity had a political basis. The Greek historian, Polybius, writing about a hundred years after Nossis, claimed that at Locri, aristocrats traced their descent through their mother's line.[9] Modern commentators have found proof of this in Nossis' description of her mother as 'Theophilis, the daughter of Cleocha' (No.79), although recently Marilyn Skinner has argued that the phrase indicates 'a gender-specific speech trait' used by all Greek women, and not just those of Locri.[10] Evidence for both theories is slight, if engaging, and Nossis' statement perhaps owes as much to her literary aspirations (Sappho also wrote a poem about three female generations),[11] than to any historical precedence, although its affirmation of women's family history in a society which more often excluded them from any such tradition, is nevertheless powerful.

Nossis also uses many other semantic forms which, if not indisputably 'gender-specific', indicate her affirmation of women's experience. For example, she twice describes the process of creating a portrait by the Greek verb *teuchein*, a word often associated with the work of women, such as weaving,[12] and in No.75 invents a new feminine diminutive noun for a puppy.[13] Marilyn Skinner has postulated that even when writing in the male persona, as in No.80, an epitaph for the comic poet Rhinthon, Nossis presents 'a female poetic persona behind the male mask', using a more feminine form, *aedonis*, for *aedon*, 'nightingale', although Rhinthon is ostensibly describing himself in the first person.[14] In addition, her epigram on a Locrian military victory,[15] seemingly out of place among so many paeans to female beauty, slyly inverts one of the standard conceits of male poetry – the grief of a dead warrior's battle-gear for their slain master.[16]

Nossis' poetic skill can stand beside that of any male writer. Like Anyte, she is a mistress of economy, weaving several themes together in four short lines. In No.82, for example, she sets up a

---

[9] Polybius, *Histories*, 12.5.9.

[10] Skinner, 1987, 39-42.

[11] See No.3.

[12] See No.75, note 28 & No.77, note 36, and in particular the *Odyssey*, 7.235, where it refers to the garments Arete has woven with her maids. Anyte uses the verb in No.63, of the grave Myro erects for her lost pets.

[13] See No.75, note 29.

[14] Skinner, 1991: 31-32

[15] No.81.

[16] See in particular, Patroclus' weeping horses in the *Iliad*, 17.426-40 & also No.81, note 49.

number of oppositions, both thematic and semantic, throughout the poem: between the virgin goddess Artemis and Alcetis, the mother in labour; between blooded arrows, and purification of blood-guilt; between Artemis washing herself 'in Inopus', and entering Alcetis' house (*es oikous*), and finally between the virgin lap of the Graces and the womb of childbirth, until a series of parallel oppositions – inside/outside, wild/domestic, virgin/mother, polluted/clean – are established. Far from 'frail trifles', as the *Oxford Classical Dictionary* would have it, this is poetry of the highest seriousness.

72: The Flowers of Love [17]

Nothing is sweeter than love. Nothing. [18]
All other delights, all pleasures come
poor second
            – the honey I have spat from my lips.

Listen. Nossis speaks: [19] whoever falls
from Cypris' favour can never know [20]
such flowers
            – roses opening, coming into bloom. [21]

---

[17] Skinner suggests, with Luck, that this epigram was composed as preface to a book of Nossis' epigrams (1991: 32), a poetic manifesto with the aim of forestalling 'the censure of a hostile reading public'.

[18] **sweeter than love**: This echoes Sappho No.1 (II).

[19] **Nossis speaks**: Like Corinna in No.34, & Sulpicia in No.88, Nossis proudly names herself in her poem (see also Nos.79, 83, 95, 97, 98 & Introduction p.12).

[20] **Cypris favour**: Locri was a cult centre for the worship of Aphrodite, the Cyprian goddess, who appears frequently in Nossis' poems.

[21] **flowers...roses opening, coming into bloom**: Roses were sacred to both the Muses (see Sappho LP 53 / Balmer No.103) and Aphrodite (see Sappho LP 2 / Balmer No.79). As such they also had erotic associations, as both gifts between lovers (see Sappho LP 94 / Balmer No.32) and in Hellenistic poetry, as Heather White has noticed (1980: 19-20), as a trope for female genitalia. Although commentators have long quarrelled over which association has ascendancy here (see Gow & Page, 1965: 435-36; Snyder, 1989: 78; Skinner 1991: 33), it seems likely that Nossis' text admits all three. Interestingly, a study by Alicia Ostriker of flower imagery in modern women's poetry found that, while retaining their 'gender identification', flowers denoted not frailty but force (1980: 256-60).

[22] **Life-Like Portraits**: See Anyte 51 & 64, note 44.

[23] **Polyarchis**: The name means 'much-ruler'.

[24] **a share...won**: Nossis' verb here is more usually used in a male context – *epauresthai* ('to partake of') found in Homer of the different heroic qualities enjoyed by warriors (*Iliad*, 13.733).

Life-Like Portraits[22]

73: Polyarchis[23]

Come with me to Aphrodite's shrine,
see her statue worked with beaten gold:
– Polyarchis set it here –
a share of many many prizes won[24]
with her body's own far-shining glory.[25]

74: Sabaethis

From far off it seems so like, a second Sabaethis;[26]
yes, this is what we all know – her beauty,
                              her body's splendour.

Look again. Close now: a new gentleness, such wisdom;[27]
so fare well, my lady, in all you do,
                              sacred to the gods.

---

[25] **her body's own...glory**: Nossis uses another Homeric word, *aglaia*, or 'splendour', applied to the battle-glory of warriors. For the possessive ('her own'), she employs an interesting adjective *oikeios*, which means literally 'belonging to a household', or 'of the domestic' – perhaps ironically applied to a woman who lived outside such conventions.

[26] **Sabaethis**: Like Polyarchis, likely to be a prostitute. The following four epigrams celebrate portraits painted on terracotta or wooden plaques, called *pinakes* and dedicated to Aphrodite. Sarah Pomeroy has come up with the novel suggestion that they could have been 'advertisements' to attract male paying customers (see Skinner, 1991: 42, note 22).

[27] **gentleness...wisdom**: As well as pointing to Sabaethis' physical beauty, Nossis also emphasises her spiritual attributes. In the *Odyssey*, Penelope – the archetypal faithful wife – is also praised for her wisdom (see Skinner, 1991: 29).

75: Thaumareta

It casts her spell so well,[28] her dignity, her growing charm –
all the wide-eyed beauty of such tender youth.
Thaumareta, if your watch-house dog, that little puppy,[29]
could see you now, she would wag her tail in joy;
the great mistress of the mansion, hers again.[30]

76 Callo [31]

Fair portrait for fairest Aphrodite's home,
Callo's own drawn likeness, her one known equal.
How still it stands –
                    her grace so softly blooming:[32]
Fare Well. Take pleasure.[33] Live out your flawless life.[34]

---

[28] **casts her spell**: Nossis uses the Greek verb *teuchein*, often used of women's handiwork (see p.84).

[29] **your little puppy**: Nossis here coins a word, *skulakaina*, a feminine diminutive of *skulax*, the Greek for 'puppy'. The ending, -*aina*, was favoured by Athenian comic playwrights such as Aristophanes and adds to the poem's teasing humour (see Skinner, 1991: 42-43, note 29).

[30] **great mistress of the mansion**: Nossis has been criticised by Gow & Page for her 'stilted' language here (1965: 440), whereas Skinner reads a criticism of Thaumareta's overweening pride (1991: 28). However, Nossis' use of grand Homeric language throughout this epigram only seems gently mocking – as much at the pretensions of epic as at her young subject's pretensions to grandeur, comparable, perhaps, to Gerty MacDowell's inner monologue in the 'Nausicaa' section of James Joyce's *Ulysses* (see Introduction p.14).

[31] **Callo**: Like Polyarchis (No.73) & Sabaethis (No.74), Callo was probably a prostitute.

[32] **grace**: The Greek word *charis* includes both physical and spiritual beauty. In the *Iliad*, it is also used of a sexual favour (see 11.243) – a reading which surely did not escape Nossis here.

[33] **Take pleasure**: Again, the Greek verb *chairein* includes a sense of sensual pleasure (see Sappho LP 96 / Balmer No.33).

[34] **flawless life**: Some commentators have taken this line to indicate that a 'flawless' Callo therefore could not have been a prostitute (see Snyder, 1989: 80). However, Nossis here links the perfect likeness of Callo with a statement about her moral worth, as in No.74, interweaving physical and spiritual attributes.

77: Melinna [35]

Melinna herself stands recreated here: [36]
    looks down on us and smiles, soft and sweet; [37]
the image of her mother – living proof
    that child is equal to her parent. [38]

Gifts for Goddesses

78: Samytha's Net

See Aphrodite's pleasure in Samytha's gift
      – a net from her soft, now-tumbling hair; [39]
so cunningly designed, [40] and that trace of nectar
      – fine ointment for some fair Adonis. [41]

---

[35] **Melinna**: Echoed in the name of a woman poet of unknown date (see No.86) – and by the name Melinna in an inscription (see No.109).

[36] **recreated**: Nossis again uses the verb *teuchein*, to weave or work (see No.75, note 28), here setting up an association, as Skinner notes (1991: 28), between women's creativity and the bearing of children.

[37] **soft and sweet**: Nossis uses the adverb *meilicios* ('gently') also found in Sappho.

[38] **child equal to her parent**: A second or third-century Pythagorean text on female chastity claims 'a woman's greatest glory...is the likeness [her children] will bear to their father' – as living proof of the legitimacy of male heirs (Lefkowitz & Fant, 1982: 104). This line neatly appropriates the sentiment for the relationship of mother and daughter (see Skinner, 1991: 28).

[39] **net**: The Greek word *kekruphalos* can mean either a 'hair-net' or 'hunting-net' – a play on Samytha's search for young lovers – or clients. The conceit of love as a chase also appears in Sappho No.8 & Sulpicia No.92.

[40] **cunningly-designed**: Nossis also uses a form of the Greek word *daidaleos* to describe Polyarchis' statue in No.73, but it is particularly fitting here with its reference to Daedalus, the famous craftsman of Greek myth, and designer of Minos' maze – another 'net'.

[41] **fair Adonis**: After Adonis' death, Aphrodite anointed his body with oils (see Anyte No.58, note 30). However, oils were also used by lovers (see Sappho LP 94 / Balmer No.32) and 'Adonis' was used as a nickname for young bucks in New Comedy, establishing a 'sly correlation' between Samytha and her clients, and Aphrodite and her young lover (Skinner, 1991: 25).

79: Three Generations [42]

Lady Hera,[43] come down to us, to your scented shrine [44]
near heaven, look with favour on our fine-stitched fabric;
with her noble daughter Nossis for new apprentice
Theophilis wove it, the daughter of Cleocha – [45]
daughter, mother, grandmother, united in the thread.

80: At Rhinthon's Tomb [46]

Break into laughter as you pass me by [47]
and then make your final fond farewell:
      I am Rhinthon, of Syracuse,
one small songbird for the Muses' strains
but slowly, slowly, from soaring satire,
      I have plucked out my own great crown.[48]

---

[42] **Three Generations**: This poem echoes Sappho's celebration of her mother and daughter (No.3), but here linked not by a luxury from overseas, but by their own handiwork.

[43] **Hera**: Again, compare Sappho's prayer to Hera (LP 17 / Balmer No.91); Hera is particularly relevant here as the goddess of family life and childbirth (see Barnard, 1978: 212).

[44] **scented shrine**: Hera's shrine was at Lacinium, a promontory near Croton, north of Locris.

[45] **Theophilis...the daughter of Cleocha**: More usually, women were identified by their father's name, although on the basis of Nossis' expression here, some commentators, both ancient and modern, believe women may have called themselves by their mothers' names when speaking to each other, either at Locri alone, or throughout the Greek world (Skinner, 1987; see p.84).

[46] **At Rhinthon's Tomb**: Rhinthon of Syracuse also lived in the early third century BC and wrote 38 plays, all burlesques of tragedies, none of which survives.

[47] **pass me by**: The Greek verb *parameibein* is particularly loaded: it could mean 'to leave on one side', 'to change or alter', or 'to pass over or omit to mention', and was also used of time passing, all of which resonate here.

[48] **my own great crown**: Nossis attests the importance of 'lesser' as well as of greater artists, of those who make us laugh as well as cry. However, as only the smallest scraps of Rhinthon's work now survive, it is Nossis' own poem which has secured his 'crown'.

81: Temple Offerings

Bruttian shields from brutish shoulders,[49]
of soldiers slain by Locri's heroes –
       swift-spoiling for a fight –
now hymn the courage of their captors
in all our towering temple shrines,
with no longing left[50] for those lost arms –
       deserters now deserted.

82: A Prayer[51]

Artemis of Delos and fair Ortygia,[52]
lay down your bow, put your arrows in the lap
of the virgin Graces;[53] wash your body clean
in Inopus' pure stream,[54] and enter this house:
release Alcetis from the pain of giving birth.

---

[49] **Bruttian...brutish**: The Greek puns on *Brettioi*, a tribe of Southern Italy and its supposed derivation from an Italian dialect word for a runaway slave or rebel (see Skinner, 1991: 31). Heavy shields were jettisoned by deserters from battle to speed flight, as Archilochus' infamous farewell to his shield illustrates (frag. 5). Nossis here echoes and inverts Archilochus, with her shields only too happy to rid themselves of their owners rather than vice versa.

[50] **longing**: Nossis uses the verb *pothein*, often used in Sappho of erotic desire.

[51] Nossis' authorship of this poem has sometimes been disputed. Artemis also features in the poetry of Sappho and Telesilla (Nos.8 & 35).

[52] **Delos and Ortygia**: These references emphasise Artemis' role as a goddess of childbirth: Artemis was born to Leto on Ortygia and then helped with the birth of her brother, Apollo, on Delos (see Snyder, 1989: 83).

[53] **Graces**: Three goddesses of beauty and charm, the companions of Aphrodite.

[54] **Inopus**: A river on Delos.

83: Nossis' Farewell [55]

Stranger, if you should sail to Mytilene,[56] city of fair song,[57]
enticed by Sappho's fragrant garland, its heady bloom,
say only this: that the land of Locri gave me life,
long-treasured by the Muses and by Her.
One more thing: My name is Nossis.[58]

Now go.

---

[55] **Nossis' Farewell**: Both Skinner & Snyder believe this was the final poem or epilogue to Nossis' collection (1991: 34; 1989: 79). Skinner also notes its similarities to a poem by Sappho (LP 96 / Balmer No.33), and to the *propempticon* genre (see Erinna No.44), although here it is a stranger rather than a friend who undertakes the journey.

[56] **Mytilene**: The main city on Lesbos, and Sappho's home.

[57] **city of fair song**: Nossis uses the Homeric epithet *kallichoros*, also employed by Corinna (see No.21, note 44).

[58] **My name is Nossis**: Here Nossis characterises herself as one of Sappho's companions, such as Atthis or Gongyla, always mentioned by name in Sappho's poetry (see Introduction p.12).

MELINNO

Melinno is known only by her one extant poem, a Greek hymn to the goddess Roma, quoted by Stobaeus in the early fifth century AD, and like Corinna, her date is the subject of much dispute, with suggestions varying by over four hundred years. Maurice Bowra has argued that the poem's awe of Roman power was a common sentiment in the early second century BC, and that its failure to name an emperor would support such an early date. Hugh Lloyd-Jones, on the other hand, believes the work to date from the second century AD, seeing in it the 'banal' style of that period's Greek revivalism (a banality he also finds in the work of Julia Balbilla).[1]

Whatever its date, Melinno's poem is unusual for its five Sapphic stanzas, hardly used since Sappho's day, which led Stobaeus to believe she came from Lesbos, although her highly artificial literary dialect, with only a few Lesbian forms, suggests this is unlikely.[2] She has been criticised for the stiffness of her poetry, dividing each stanza into a self-contained unit of thought, unlike Sappho or her male contemporary Alcaeus, destroying the fluidity of their earlier poetry. However, Bowra suggested that the poem might have been composed for a ritual purpose, sung at five different 'stations', and so necessitating its rigorous divisions.[3]

Even Melinno's apologists point to her lack of poetic distinction, detailing her turgid style and epic stiffness. Yet, if stilted, her poem is more complex than might at first appear, fusing standard poetic conceits to create an original whole, a Greek poetic incarnation for a Roman ideal.[4] Like Anyte, her work is rich with literary allusion, as well as mythological reference, betraying a high degree of learning. As Bowra comments, her poetry displays 'its own character and conviction'.[5]

---

[1] Bowra, 1970: 211; Lloyd-Jones, see Pomeroy, 1977: 57. See Nos.94-97.

[2] See Bowra, 1970: 199. Bowra also notes that the name 'Melinna' appears in Nossis (see No.77).

[3] Bowra, 1970: 201; see Pindar's *Olympian* 5 which was divided into self-contained triads for the same purpose.

[4] See No.84, notes 8 & 10.

[5] Bowra, 1970: 212.

84: Melinno's Hymn to Roma[6]

Hail to Roma, the war-god's daughter
warrior queen in a golden girdle,[7]
your Heaven here on earth, eternal
and unassailable.

On you alone, our ancient of days,
Fate has bestowed this royal glory
of unbroken rule, sovereign strength
to lead where all follow.[8]

For under your yoke, by your strong reins,
the great back of earth and foam-white seas
are bent; without a falter you steer
the cities of all men.[9]

But time's great span can topple us all;
life sways us one way, then another
you alone sail on fair winds of rule
and never alter course.[10]

For you alone have borne strong warriors,
great spearman, springing up unbidden
like Demeter's fruitful ears of corn,
a crop of mortal men.[11]

---

[6] **Roma**: The goddess Roma, a personification of Rome's power, was often celebrated in Greek poetry, although this is one of the few to survive (see No.114).

[7] **war-god's daughter**: Ares, a fitting parent for such a pugnacious offspring. He was also father to the Amazon Penthesilea, and here Melinno characterises Roma as an Amazon warrior; her golden girdle a symbol of strength and power (see Bowra, 1970: 202-03).

[8] **Fate…**: The idea that Rome had an unstoppable destiny is found in the Greek historian Polybius (*Histories*, 1.4.4)

[9] This echoes the second chorus of Sophocles' tragedy *Antigone* (308ff).

[10] Melinno sets up a traditional Greek sentiment – the mutability of time – and then makes Rome the contradiction to prove the rule. She also merges two standard poetic conceits; the winds of fortune and the ship of state.

[11] **a crop of mortal men**: Melinno compares the Romans with the *Spartoi* ('sown men'), the mythological warrior-race of Thebes who sprang from the ground after Cadmus sowed dragon's teeth, comparing them to harvested corn.

SULPICIA

Sulpicia has been identified as the ward, possibly even the niece, of M. Valerius Messalla Corvinus (64 BC – AD 8),[1] an eminent literary patron during the time of the emperor Augustus. She was probably a member of a poetic circle which included the male elegist Tibullus, amongst whose work her poems, also written in the elegiac form, have been preserved. Over the centuries, scholars have debated the authorship of these works, firstly attributing them all to Tibullus, and later dividing them into two distinct groups:[2] those by Sulpicia,[3] and those written about Sulpicia by an unknown male author (the so-called *auctor de Sulpicia*),[4] two of which employ her own poetic persona 'as though,' one scholar comments, 'he wanted to show her how it could have been done'.[5] This orthodoxy has recently been challenged by Holt Parker, who argues that the many semantic and thematic similarities between Sulpicia's work and those supposedly written in her voice, as well as the relative unlikeliness of any male poet undertaking such an obscure exercise,[6] should restore those two poems at least, to Sulpicia's authorship – an attribution I have followed here.[7]

Sulpicia's reputation, too, has suffered, with even the feminist historian, Sarah Pomeroy, declaring 'her work... of interest only because the author is female'.[8] Following the common assumption that women's art is usually biographical, scholars have sniffed at 'sincere' or 'spontaneous', even 'amateur' poems, with one translator conjuring up 'the naive young girl suddenly growing up to complexity of thought as she grapples with the ideas love has forced on her'.[9]

Such 'complexity of thought' has proved the real difficulty for commentators: Sulpicia's breath-taking constructions, piling clause on clause, argument on argument, have left many scholars far behind, grumbling of feminine illogic, even an inferior 'distaff'

---

[1] See Haupt, 1871: 32-34.
[2] Gruppe, 1838: I, 25-64; see Lowe, 1988: 194-95.
[3] Tibullus, 3.13-18.
[4] Tibullus, 3.8-12.
[5] Tibullus, 3.9 & 3.11; Luck, 1969: 109.
[6] But see West's view on Erinna's 'Distaff' (No.42).
[7] Parker, 1994; Nos.91 & 92.
[8] Pomeroy, 1975: 173.
[9] Dunlop, 1972: 54; see Santirocco, 1979: 231 & Lefkowitz, 1981a: 59-68; Balmer, 1992: 7-8.

Latin, 'where the words yield grammatical sense only under duress and the meaning is likewise uncertain... impervious to analysis by rigorous linguistic method'.[10] N.J. Lowe, however, has pointed out that such criticisms raise interesting questions about Sulpicia's work – as they do of all classical women's poetry.[11] Sulpicia's much-noted colloquialisms, for instance, echo a testimony by Cicero that aristocratic Roman women spoke a language loaded with 'archaisms', a reference, perhaps, to the colloquial expressions found in the early comedies of Plautus or Terence, whose dialogues, it has been claimed, can be distinguished by the gender of their speaker.[12] Certainly, Sulpicia's syntax, as Lowe has shown, differs from that of her male contemporaries; for while her teasing word-play and extraordinary internal and end rhymes, however dazzling, are echoed by the skill of other Latin elegists such as Propertius and Ovid, her densely intertwined constructions of thought, layered one on the other – paradox on paradox, reversal on reversal, surprise on surprise – are unique.

Sulpicia's thematic concerns, too, both echo and contradict those of the male elegists. In Propertius 1.3., for instance, the poet's lover, Cynthia, bewails a night of languid misery, trying to pass the time until he returned to her 'from some other woman's door'. In No.88, 'Sulpicia Angry,' Sulpicia proudly declares her determination not to be humiliated by an errant lover. Similarly, Sulpicia's description of her overwhelming passion in No.91, 'Sulpicia's Advice to a Lover on His Birthday', echoes Dido's words in Ovid's *Heroides* (7.23-30), with both protagonists declaring *uror*: 'I burn'.[13] Yet where Ovid concentrates on the pain Dido suffers over Aeneas' desertion, Sulpicia quickly moves on to the hope that Cerinthus, too, will share her intensity. And while Dido prays that Venus will 'surrender' Aeneas to her,[14] Sulpicia demands that love should be a mutual slavery; if not then she will withdraw her suit.

This mischievous insistence on the equality of relations between the sexes informs all of Sulpicia's poetry, providing an invaluable and precious glimpse into the emotional consciousness of Roman women, seen elsewhere only through the distorted mirror of the male elegists' often sub-pornographic characterisations.[15] Her sexual

---

[10] Gruppe, 1838: 49-50.

[11] See Lowe, 1988: 195 & Introduction pp.15-16.

[12] Lowe, 1988: 195; Cicero, *On Oration*, 3.45; see No.86, note 23 & No.89, note 33.

[13] See No.91, note 36.

[14] *Heroides*, 7.31-34

honesty, her witty sensuality and teasing innuendo, too, present an image of womanhood far from the traditional 'silent women' of Rome.[16] Most of all it is her mental agility which impresses, the semantic complexities which, whether determined by gender or not, are nevertheless essential features of her 'distinctive poetic imagination'.[17] No wonder Ezra Pound, for one, found her poetry 'worth ten years of a man's life to translate'.[18]

---

[15] For a study of the gender constructions of Roman elegy, see Hallett: 1993.

[16] See Finley, 1968.

[17] Lowe, 1988: 205.

[18] Pound, 1929/30.

85: Sulpicia in Love

At last love has come along, and now it seems my greater shame
to cover up than bare all,[19] or so I should believe.
For Venus heard my plaintive song, settled all outstanding claims –
bound him over,[20] dropped him in my lap, and up my sleeve.
Love's promise is fulfilled: so let them publicise my pleasures
– if they've none, that is, to speak of, nothing of their own.
No, I won't bring my soul to book, seal up my secret treasures
in case some other lover might take them out on loan.
To err is divine; to change heart – and minds – surely asinine;
shout it loud: for this worthy woman, a worthwhile man.

---

[19] **cover up...bare all**: Throughout the poem Sulpicia sets up a series of witty oppositions between reputations, good, bad, rumoured, and literary. Here, she also uses a clothing metaphor through the verbs *tegere* 'to conceal' or 'to clothe', and *nudare* 'to expose' or 'to strip bare', allowing the opportunity for more teasing double meanings.

[20] **plaintive song...outstanding claims...bound over**: Sulpicia's Latin here is loaded with legal overtones (see Introduction p.16, note 48).

86: Sulpicia Thwarted [21]

Hateful birthday, here again, and I must pass a tedious
tearful trip to the country – all without Cerinthus.
For what's more charming than the city? Is a draughty villa
fit for the girl about town? Arno's freezing river? [22]
Too much now, Messalla, you're stifling me – give this girl a rest, [23]
since travel, uncle, does not broaden every mind.
For if my body's carried off, [24] then I'll leave my thoughts behind,
since you won't let me judge what I know – or love – the best. [25]

87: Sulpicia Saved

Have you heard, I've been released? Yes, the weight of that dull
journey
has been lifted from your girl, freed from rural humdrum
to celebrate her birthday in Rome; a treat for all which comes
to you by surprise, my love – and with it, of course, me.

---

[21] This pair of poems, on a lover's unwilling journey proposed then abandoned, is echoed in Propertius (1.8a & b), although in Propertius, the poet is the forsaken lover, first concerned at the distractions his mistress, Cynthia, might find abroad, and later delighted at her decision to remain in Rome, swayed by the power of his poetic persuasion. Some commentators, too, have seen a cause and effect in Sulpicia's two poems, with her guardian Messalla won over by her literary pleading (see Santirocco, 1979: 232).

[22] **Arno's freezing river**: A river in Etruria near Rome where Sulpicia's family presumably had their country estate. Sulpicia describes it as *frigidus*, which, like English 'frigid', also had sexual connotations. Sulpicia's language here is in marked opposition to the heat or *fervor* of her other poems (see Nos.89, 90 & 91).

[23] **give... a rest**: The Latin verb *quiescere* or 'to rest', 'to keep quiet' has a similar colloquial meaning to English (see Plautus, *Mostellaria*, 5.2.51).

[24] **carried off**: Sulpicia uses the verb *abducere*, which has a particular frisson when used by a woman, as it also means 'to carry away forcibly' or 'rape'.

[25] This line has caused some problems of interpretation, but Sulpicia's syntactical ambiguity here echoes her state of mind – an ambiguity maintained in the translation.

88: Sulpicia Angry

Here's a pleasant thought: now you've become so careless over me
there's no sad chance that I might take a sudden tumble.[26]
So take more trouble for some rag-bag tart in tatty toga[27]
than for Sulpicia, Servius's non-servile daughter;[28]
there are those who trouble about me, those whose greatest grumble
is that I might now let it slip – and for nobody.[29]

89: Sulpicia Sick[30]

Have you no respect, Cerinthus, no concern for your sweetheart[31]
now fever fires up my feeble frame, allows no rest?
Oh, but I don't desire a cure, an end to torrid torment
if you don't want it too, won't play your own willing part.
For what good are cures, why conquer cares, if you could not care
                                                              less,[32]
can bear this heat so coolly, all your compassion spent?[33]

---

[26] **tumble**: The verb *cadere*, 'to fall', can mean 'to trip over', 'to make a mistake', and possibly, in colloquial speech, 'fall into bed' (see Smith, 1913: 513). Used by a woman, within a sexually hypocritical society, it has another edge, that of a fallen reputation.

[27] **rag-bag tart...tatty toga**: The Latin refers to the prostitute's *quasillum* or 'wool-basket', indicating her low social status as a wool-worker. Togas, too, were worn by lower-class women, and became synonymous with prostitution, although for men they were a sign of citizenship and high political office.

[28] **Sulpicia, Servius' daughter**: Like Sappho, Corinna & Nossis, Sulpicia uses her own name as a poetic strategy (see Introduction p.12), opening this sentence with *scortum*, or 'prostitute', and closing it with 'Sulpicia', while the name Servius puns ironically on the Latin for a slave – *servus*. Love as slavery was a common conceit in elegiac poetry (see No.91).

[29] **let it slip...for nobody**: The Latin puns on the verb *cedere*, 'to give way to', 'to lose one's place to' or 'to yield to' – with a definite sexual overtone – neatly paralleling and phonically echoing *cadere* of line 1. Commentators have fretted over the ambiguity of the sense (see Snyder, 1989: 133; Lowe, 1988: 200-01) – whether Sulpicia is saying she won't let her rival steal her lover or won't let her lover steal her 'honour'; her complex Latin admits both readings.

100

90: Sulpicia Sorry

Don't carry a burning torch for me, my love, my fierce bright light,
– as I thought perhaps you might have done these past few days –
if I have ever done anything more foolish in my life,
anything I could confess to you that might outweigh
this grievous greatest crime of leaving you alone late last night
desiring only to disguise my own red-hot blaze.[34]

[30] **Sulpicia Sick**: The conceit of love as a fever was common in elegiac poetry.

[31] **respect...concern**: Sulpicia asks Cerinthus to show her *pia cura*, or 'dutiful concern' an echo of the *pietas* or 'sense of duty' Catullus found in his love for Lesbia, the key moral value of the Augustan age (see Santirroco, 1979: 233).

[32] **care less**: The Latin contains a brilliant pun in *si tu* – 'if you' and *situ* 'with neglect' (see Ovid's *perire situ* 'to die of neglect' in *Amores*, 2.3.14).

[33] **all compassion spent**: The Latin, *lento pectore ferre*, means literally 'to bear with a light heart', but was used metaphorically as 'calmly' or 'dispassionately' (see Cicero, *On Oratory*, 2.45.190), which gave me my translation here.

[34] This poem contains one sentence in Latin – a tortuous and complex series of subordinated clauses within clauses. The light/fire imagery can also be found in Nos.89 & 91.

91: Sulpicia's Advice to a Lover on His Birthday [35]

This festive day, Cerinthus, this day which delivered you to me,
will be sacred forever, our own blazing portent.
For when you were born the cruel Fates cried down fresh slavery
on women, made you harsh overseer, searing torment.
And I burn more than most. [36] But I'll take my pleasure on those coals,
Cerinthus, if my fierce fires can somehow fire you too;
on our tender tinder love, and to your own slow-sparking soul, [37]
I'm praying that this same desire will catch hold in you.

So I'll make the sacrifice, birth spirit, fan his dying flame;
you turn his thoughts to mine, make his body yearn for mine.
But if by chance he's smouldering at the sound of some new name,
then leave his hearth-fires smoking, desert that faithless shrine.
And you Venus, play us fair; either forge us both together
slave to branded slave, or release me from my bondage –
no better make it together, and with your strongest fetter,
the links not even time can corrode or disengage.

You see, the man has his wants but still stays silent as he's wont,
too ashamed (so far) to speak those three small words out loud.
But in my brazen birthday suit, my love, here's my binding vow:
you'll be damned if you do, but damned (by me) if you don't.

---

[35] This poem is often thought to have been written by the so-called *auctor de Sulpicia* – an unknown male poet writing in her poetic voice (see above p.95). However, its teasing confidence, exquisite word-play and championship of the woman's cause in love strongly echo Sulpicia's other poems; I therefore followed Holt Parker (1994) in restoring it to her authorship. For a contemporary woman poet's witty list of instructions about her lover, see Wendy Cope's 'My Lover' (in France, 1993: 89-91).

[36] **I burn more than most**: In the six hundred years since Sappho (see No.2), her description of the physical reaction of the lover to the loved one had become standard. Here, Sulpicia humorously claims that she is more inflamed than other women.

[37] **to your... soul**: On Cerinthus' birthday, Sulpicia invokes his '*Genius*' or daemon – his guiding spirit – in the conventional appeal for a deity to intercede between poet and loved one.

92: To Cerinthus at the Hunt³⁸

Don't toy with my boy, ugly boar, as you roam the great outdoors,
poring over crooked paths, your hidden mountain lairs –
and please, don't think to sharpen those tough old tusks; this
      isn't war:
Love, protect him for me, just return him unimpaired;
for he's been captured for the chase, and Diana's all the rage³⁹
(oh those dark woods can pine away, hounds go to the dogs).
What frenzy's this, what sort of scheme, to use forests for a cage
or wound those oh so supple hands, give self-harm the nod?
And what pleasure's here, among wild beasts, to penetrate their hides,
brand with thorns those milk-white thighs, endure such stinging barbs?
So here's the plan, Cerinthus, clear: let me wander by your side,
bear your tangled, twisted webs along such shady paths;
yes, I can rake the cooling traces, track down your own fast deer,
slip the leash, unchain the dog, swoon at the scent of hare
(oh these dark woods can give such pleasure, if you, my light, stay near).
So let's make love – to prove the point – by the sets and snares;
and we'll let wild beasts walk by our mesh, retire again intact
(crashing boars could never jolt the joy of our caress).
But don't play Venus without me, make Diana's virgin pact:
be chaste, not chased, my own true boy, cast your purest nets.
And if some girl should stalk my love, mark him out for secret prey,
then let the beasts tear out her heart, you just cut her charms;
the chase's thrill is not for you, leave your father to the fray,
except, of course, for this charge – into my waiting arms.

---

³⁸ Like No.90, this poem, too, is usually accredited to the *auctor de Sulpicia*; for the same reasons, I have restored it to Sulpicia (see No.90, note 35).

³⁹ **Diana's all the rage**: One of Sulpicia's neat paradoxes – she complains that Diana, as patron of the hunt, is now Cerinthus' only obsession, but later asks him to embrace her lifestyle as the goddess of chastity (see Sappho 8, note 41).

SULPICIA THE SATIRIST

The second Sulpicia, amongst some stiff competition, is probably the most shadowy figure of all the classical women poets. Even a recent study of ancient women writers relegates her to a footnote,[1] and feminist studies have often focused on her incarnation as a character in the poetry of the satirist Martial.[2] Like Martial, she lived in Rome during the reign of Domitian (AD 81-96), and although a seventy-line hexameter poem satirising Domitian's expulsion of philosophers from Rome was once attributed to her, it is now known to be a fourth-century fraud (on the basis, if nothing else, that no one would have been foolish enough to satirise Domitian during his lifetime). A two-line fragment from a seemingly erotic work, however, has survived, first in a work by one 'Probus', a scholiast on Juvenal, now also lost, but quoted in turn by an Italian Renaissance scholar, Giorgio Valla of Piacenza (c. 1430-99).[3]

With such a complex pedigree, it is perhaps surprising that even two lines have been preserved, especially, as Amy Richlin points out, given the enthusiastic purges of classical texts by medieval monasteries.[4] For although Martial's 'Sulpicia' is portrayed as risqué, writing of 'games, delights and laughter,' she celebrates only 'chaste and proper loves', that is, between man and wife.[5] Our fragment, on the other hand, although the subject of much critical dispute, appears to suggest a rather more liberal approach, as the poet recalls a night of intense sexual activity, seeing herself 'stripped bare'. The satirist's teasing concision and ambiguity echoes that of her earlier namesake, as too, perhaps, does her use of unusual linguistic forms.[6] Richlin has even argued that it seems too much of a coincidence for two of the very few extant Roman women writers to share the same name, suggesting that Sulpicia

---

[1] Snyder, 1989: 175, note 14.
[2] See Hallett, 1993.
[3] See Parker, 1992: 89.
[4] Richlin, 1992: 138.
[5] Martial, *Satires*, 10.35, 8-9.
[6] See No.93, note 12.
[7] Richlin, 1992: 138. Interestingly, another Sulpicia, Sulpicia Lepidina, is known through her correspondence with Claudia Severa, the wife of a prefect at Vindolanda on Hadrian's Wall; Claudia's letters were recently excavated at the fort (see Introduction p.16, note 45).

the elegist might have been a 'literal' as well as literary foremother of the later poet.[7]

Despite the eroticism of Sulpicia's satire, she was nevertheless held in high regard by later writers. Ausonius, for example, listed her alongside Plato and Juvenal, and a late fifth-century poet, Sidonius Apollinaris, calls her playful jokes 'inimitable'.[8] Sulpicia's tiny fragment, is invaluable to us, too; a unique example of a woman straddling two almost exclusively male genres – satire and erotic verse. At the same time, it offers an explicit celebration of female desire, appropriating, as Richlin notes, 'the male gaze' of traditional Latin poetry as Sulpicia looks down at herself lying naked with her lover.[9]

---

[8] Ausonius, *Wedding Cento*, 139.5-6; Sidonius Apollinaris, *Songs*, 9.261-62.
[9] Richlin, 1992: 139; see Parker, 1992: 92-93.

93: The Morning After [10]

If we could only set it straight, restore that sagging mattress – [11]
then you'd see me stripped, laid bare, entwined with Calenus. [12]

---

[10] **The Morning After**: Sulpicia's fragment contains only half a sentence which begins but does not end a conditional phrase ('if only…'). Its meaning has been the subject of intense debate with three main interpretations emerging: (I) the poem's central image represents a metaphor for the marriage-bed, disturbed by an argument, which Sulpicia hopes will soon be resolved (Morel, 1963: 134, cited by Parker, 1992: 93); (II) the same image refers literally to the bed disturbed by 'the intensity of her love-making' (Parker, ibid); (III) the fragment originates from a satire on marriage written from a woman's point of view, with its unfinished clause completed by something like 'Then you'd see what it's really like!' (Richlin, 1992: 132). Here I have tried to reflect the ambiguity of interpretation, but closed the conditional in the interests of clarity.

[11] **sagging mattress**: The Latin uses the specific term *fasciis cadurci*, 'the mattress straps', which fixed it to the bed-stead; *cadurcum* was a kind of bedding-linen named after its makers, the Gallic tribe of the Cadurci. The line is echoed in Juvenal *Satire*, 6.537, which refers to a mattress 'polluted' by sex on a religious day of abstinence. The scholiast on Juvenal, who also quoted this fragment (see p.104), notes that *cadurcum* was also used of female genitalia, while Parker points to the 'masculine' language of Sulpicia here, 'neither primary obscenities or coy euphemisms' (see Parker, 1992: 93-94).

[12] **entwined with Calenus**: Richlin notes Sulpicia's 'innovative' verb form – *concubantem*, or 'lying with for intercourse' (1992: 132). Calenus was the name of Sulpicia's husband in Martial's *Satires*.

JULIA BALBILLA

Graffiti might seem an unlikely source for classical women's poetry, but Julia Balbilla's four verses, scratched on the left foot of Memnon's huge statue on the banks of the Nile near Thebes in Egypt, were commissioned, so she tells us, by the emperor Hadrian himself.[1] Julia was accompanying Hadrian's wife, the empress Sabina, on a visit to Egypt in AD 130 – the fateful trip during which Hadrian's young favourite, Antinous, was drowned in the Nile.[2] The stones of the 'colossi' of Memnon, said to 'sing' at dawn, were one of the biggest draws for ancient tourists to Egypt, as they still are today. Visiting around the first century BC, the geographer Strabo was unsure whether the noise emanated from the statue itself, or from the people around it,[3] although the phenomenon is now believed to have been caused by the sun's rays warming the cracked stone and causing it to 'hum'.[4] The singing continued until the early third century AD, when the stones were repaired by the emperor Septimius Severus.[5]

Little is known of Julia outside her work, but in one of her poems she celebrates her illustrious ancestry, referring to her maternal and paternal grand-fathers, 'Balbillus' and 'Antiochus'.[6] Antiochus is believed to be Antiochus IV, King of Commagene, a district of Syria (reigning from AD 38-72), and out of several candidates, Balbillus has been identified as Tiberius Claudius Balbillus, the learned astronomer who became Prefect of Egypt under Nero in AD 55.[7]

Julia's poems, as Bernand has noted,[8] are also extremely erudite, written in Aeolic, the dialect of Sappho, but by now a highly artificial literary language, and containing rare words and Homeric

---

[1] See No.96.

[2] Baldson believes Antinous was still alive during the visit to Memnon (1962: 140), although Marguerite Yourcenar in her novel *Memoirs of Hadrian*, places his death immediately before the incident (1986: 172).

[3] Strabo, *Geography*, 13 & 17.

[4] McGrath, 1982: 174.

[5] Compare the seventeenth-century 'weeping' effigy of Edward Cooke in St Bartholomew's, Smithfield, London, a phenomenon caused by condensation, which ceased after new heating was installed in the church in the 1960s.

[6] No.95.

[7] See Bernand, 1960: 92.

[8] See Bernand: 84.

echoes,[9] although over the centuries, her work has become a by-word for poetic banality, even amongst feminist scholars.[10] Yet her poems contain some excellent literary devices, from internal rhyme to stirring metaphor. And if technically imperfect, it should be remembered that above all, these were spontaneous compositions, written for the moment, and, it would appear, in a moment.[11] If only all graffiti were as accomplished.

[9] For a full list, see Bernand: 84.

[10] See Pomeroy, 1977: 57.

[11] Yourcenar has Hadrian refer to the 'inexhaustible Julia Balbilla' (1986: 173).

[12] 19th/20th November AD 130. Julia and Sabina's first visit to the statue results in silence, but on their return with Hadrian the following day, they hear the statue 'sing'.

[13] **Lord of All**: Hadrian.

[14] 20th November, AD 130: Julia and Sabina's second visit to the statue.

[15] **child...of Tithonus**: When Eös, the Dawn, fell in love with Tithonus, she begged Zeus to give him eternal life, but forgot to ask for eternal youth. Eventually he became so shrunken and shrivelled, he was transformed into a cicada (see Sappho LP 58 / Balmer No.31). Memnon, their son, was King of Egypt and died defending Troy against the Greeks; at his funeral a flock of birds, sent by Zeus, flew out from his pyre and were said to return to his tomb yearly.

[16] **Thebes....Zeus**: Thebes was sacred to Zeus.

[17] **Amenoth**: Memnon's statue stood at the entrance to the temple of the deified Egyptian king, Amenhotep (or 'Amenoth') III.

[18] **Cambyses**: A Persian King, who conquered Egypt in 525 BC and was believed to have dismantled Memnon's statue after his sack of Thebes (Memnon's vast head is now in the British Museum – the largest piece in their Egyptian collection).

[19] **Apis**: Herodotus tells the story of Cambyses' murder of Apis, an Egyptian god embodied in a sacred ox, which he struck with his sword in the thigh; years later he accidentally pierced his own thigh with the same sword. The wound then turned gangrenous and proved fatal (*Histories*, 3.28-30; 64).

94: On the First Day, Not Hearing Memnon [12]

Yesterday Memnon, you met His consort with silence –
a ruse to see the beauteous Sabina once again;
for in our queen's comely form you took such great pleasure.
But when she returns, cry out; give voice to the divine,
lest the Lord of All [13] be angered that for too long now
you have defied with pride his majestic wedded wife.

(At the power of mighty Hadrian, Memnon trembled,
and suddenly cried out, to Sabina's great delight.)

95: With Sabina Augusta
Before the Column of Memnon [14]

Child of the Dawn, Memnon, son of holy Tithonus, [15]
you sit hard by ancient Thebes, great citadel of Zeus, [16]
or Amenoth, [17] Egyptian king, as learned priests can tell
from tales of old, Greetings: sing out now and welcome her
with grace, the revered wife of the emperor Hadrian.
Your tongue and ears were cleaved, a Barbarian did this deed,
godless Cambyses. [18] But by that same slashing sword point,
he paid the penalty, met his certain, wretched end,
as he once slaughtered god-like Apis, [19] no pity shown.
But I do not believe your end is nigh, great statue,
your spirit saved, immortalised forever in my thoughts.
For revered is the stock from which I myself have sprung –
of Balbillus the wise, and Antiochus the king
(Balbillus fathered my mother, gave her royal blood,
and King Antiochus was father to my father) –
from this race I have gained my fair share of noble blood,
and these lines are mine, Balbilla, Julia, revered.

96: When Hadrian Augustus Heard
the Voice of Memnon[20]

Of Memnon the Egyptian I had learnt, of stones that speak,
warmed to life by the sun's rays, a voice from Theban rock.
And on seeing Hadrian, Lord of All, he greeted Him
even before first light – as far as he was able.[21]
And when Titan's white horses had charged across the sky,
plunged a second measure of the dial into shadow,[22]
Memnon cried out loud again, a clashing voice like bronze
on bronze; and for the third time he cried out in full voice.
Hadrian the emperor made him welcome with full dues
and left these lines on stone for those who might come after,
recounting all that he had seen and all he had heard:
here made manifest that he is honoured by the gods.

97: Post-script[23]

The stone then sang out, and I heard it, I, Balbilla,
heard the sacred voice of Memnon, or great Amenoth;
I had come with our beloved empress, Sabina,
just as the first hour of the day ran its final course,
in this the fifteenth year of the Emperor Hadrian,
on this the twenty-fourth day of the month of Hathyr.[24]

And on the twenty-fifth day I wrote this here in stone.

---

[20] November 20, AD 130: Julia and Sabina return with Hadrian; eventually the statue sings again.

[21] **as far as he was able**: Memnon couldn't 'speak' before sunrise.

[22] **Titan's white horses…shadow**: Titan was a name used by poets such as Ovid for the sun, characterised as a charioteer driving his horses across the sky; here as he does so, he drags the shadow across the sundial.

[23] 21st November, AD 130: Julia returns again alone and leaves a memento of her visit on the stone.

[24] **fifteenth year…twenty-fourth of Hathyr**: This identifies the date precisely as the 20th November, AD 130; Hathyr was a month in the Egyptian calendar. See Cavafy's *In the Month of Athyr*, which reconstructs an imaginary ancient funerary inscription at Alexandria (Keeley & Sherrard, 1975: 144-45).

PROBA

Faltonia Betitia Proba, from a wealthy and aristocratic Roman family, lived around the middle of the fourth century AD. Her husband, Adelphius became prefect of Rome in AD 351 and Proba wrote a poem, now lost, on the civil wars between Constantius II and the usurper Magnentius in 353. Later she converted to Christianity and undertook her masterpiece, a reworking of Virgil known as a *cento*, or 'patchwork quilt', which unravelled his epic poems such as the *Aeneid* or the *Georgics* and stitched them back together to form a new seven-hundred line poem celebrating the life of Christ.

The cento genre was nothing new (one earlier example advised on bread-baking), but Proba was one of the first writers to use it in a Christian context, and is the only early Christian woman writer whose work survives intact.[1] One scholar has suggested that her work was composed after the apostate emperor Julian issued an edict in AD 362 forbidding Christian teachers to declare classical texts sacriligious,[2] although it may have had a more general pedagogic purpose, allowing Christian sons to became familiar with the works of Virgil – still a prerequisite for a legal or public career – without fear of contamination by pagan ideology.[3] Interestingly, the Christian scholar Jerome, a younger contemporary, singled out women as authors of centos, sneeringly referring to their 'puerile' art.[4] Modern commentators, too, have been less than charitable, pointing to Proba's derivative and inept composition. But a recent study has argued that centos required more skill than might at first appear – in counting metre, ensuring agreement and suitable verb forms. In addition, originality was not a prerequisite of ancient poetry, with Virgil borrowing freely from Homer,[5] and the New Testament quoting the Old 'in essentially cento format'.[6] However, there was still room for individual expression, as the following two extracts reveal; in the first, the opening lines of her cento, Proba borrows from Virgil's *Aeneid* to make a personal statement

---

[1] Clark & Hatch, 1981: 98.
[2] A.G. Amatucci, see Clark & Hatch, 1981: 98-99.
[3] See Clark & Hatch: 100 & Heather, 1994: 182-84.
[4] See Clark & Hatch: 104-05.
[5] See No.98, note 11.
[6] See Clark & Hatch, 1981: 105.

about her work with ingenuity and style. In the second, she uses quotations from Virgil's pastoral poem, the *Georgics*, to describe God's creation of the seasons – a highly original piece, with no biblical counterpart. Both are remarkable not only for their scholarship and technical skill but, as Gillian Clark has noted, their unique integration of Christian and classical forms.[7] As a later bishop remarked, this was a woman who could stand 'among the men of the church'.[8]

[7] Clark, 1994: 137.

[8] Isidore of Seville: 5.

[9] **Once I wrote**: A reference not only to Proba's earlier military poem, but also to Virgil's words in their original context, the *Aeneid*.

[10] **cities widowed...**: From *Aeneid* 8.571, in a speech by Evander on the atrocities of his enemies.

[11] **seven-fold Spirit**: The adjective *septemplex* is used by Virgil in imitation of Homer (e.g. *Iliad*, 7.220) to describe a warrior's shield, made with seven ox-hides. It was used of the Holy Spirit by later Christian writers, such as Orosius (6.2), and occurs in the same context in the New Testament (*Revelations*, 1.4).

[12] **Proba, the prophet**: Like Sappho, Corinna, Sulpicia, Nossis and Julia Balbilla, Proba names herself in her poetry (see Introduction p.12). She describes herself as a *vatis* or 'prophet', a word also applied to divinely-inspired poets (see Snyder, 1989: 137).

98: Proba's Purpose

Once I wrote[9] of leaders violating sacred tracts,
of those who cling to their terrible thirst for power;
of so many slaughters, the cruel campaigns of Kings,
of blood-brothers at battle, illustrious shields spattered
with kindred gore, trophies taken from would-be allies,
cities widowed once again of their countless peoples:[10]
of these, I confess, I once wrote.
                            It is enough to record such evil.
Now, all-powerful God, take, I pray, my sacred song,
loosen the voices of your eternal, seven-fold
Spirit;[11] unlock the innermost chambers of my heart,
that I, Proba, the prophet,[12] might reveal its secrets.
Now I spurn the nectar of Olympus, find no joy
in calling down the Muses from their high mountain haunts;
not for me to spread the idle boast that rocks can speak,
or pursue the theme of laureled tripods, voided vows,
the brawling gods of princes, vanquished votive idols:[13]
Nor do I seek to extend my glory through mere words[14]
or court their petty praise in the vain pursuits of men.
But baptised, like the blest, in the Castalian font –[15]
I, who in my thirst have drunk libations of the Light –[16]
now begin my song:[17] be at my side, Lord, set my thoughts
straight, as I tell how Virgil sang the offices of Christ.[18]

---

[13] **vanquished votive idols**: In the *Aeneid*, the phrase *victosque Penates* is used of the Trojans' household gods, rescued from the city after its sack by the Greeks (1.68). Proba transfers it from a heroic to a scornful context, thus changing the translation of the Latin.

[14] **extend glory through...words**: In the *Aeneid*, Hercules tells Pallas his glory will be extended not by words but by *factis* or 'deeds' (10.468).

[15] **Castalian font**: A fountain on Mount Parnassus, sacred to the Muses; those who drank its waters were said to increase their poetic powers.

[16] **libations of the Light**: A reference to Proba's Christian baptism.

[17] **begin my song**: From the opening of the *Georgics* (1.5).

[18] **Virgil...Christ**: A common early Christian belief, after Virgil's *Eclogue* 4, which foretold the birth of a child who would return the world to its former paradise.

113

99: God Creates the Seasons

When He saw them all shining steadfast in such clear skies,[19]
the Almighty gave His name and number to the stars.[20]
And the year He divided into four equal parts – [21]
summer's heat, soft spring rains, the winds driving in the cold.
And so that we might know each season by their own signs,
the earth swells up with Spring, cries out for nourishing seed,
the grain lies parched in the midday heat on threshing-floors;
Autumn lays out its fruits, one by one, and darkness comes
with Winter, black berries trodden down by olive press.
And so the year turns over and over on itself,
traces the tracks it has laid many times before...

---

[19] This line is taken from the *Aeneid*, a description of the Trojan hero Palinurus at the helm of their ship (3.518).

[20] In the *Georgics*, sailors, under the benign rule of Jove, name and number the stars for themselves (1.137).

[21] **divided into four equal parts**: From *Georgics* 1.258, although Proba is also referring to *Genesis*, 1.14.

EUDOCIA

The empress Eudocia was born *c.* AD 400, at the very end of the Roman empire, the daughter of the Athenian pagan sophist, Leontius, and like her father, was said to be versed in astronomy, philosophy, mathematics and literature. In 421 she married the emperor Theodosius II and converted to Christianity. However in 442 or 443, she separated from Theodosius in shadowy circumstances, with her biographer, Malalas, offering an unlikely story in which she was banished due to a misunderstanding over an uneaten apple. Recent historians have seen in the tale a complex web of internecine court intrigue in which Eudocia, wittingly or unwittingly, was trapped.[1] Whatever the reason, she settled in Jerusalem, founding part of the city's wall at Mount Zion and the church of Siloam, enjoying a social, if celibate, life until her death in AD 460.

More certain is Eudocia's considerable learning (Malalas tells an apparently apocryphal tale in which her father, so impressed by her grounding in philosophy, left all his fortune to her brothers, leaving her to make her own living).[2] While on a pilgrimage to Palestine around AD 438, she delivered a panegyric to the city of Antioch, and her literary works include an eight-hundred line poem on the martyrdom of St Cyprian, and, like Proba, a cento, this time in Greek, stitched from Homer's epic poems. More recently archaeologists excavating the bath-house complex at Hammat Gader in the Yarmuk Valley, Israel, have discovered a new poem by Eudocia, a seventeen-line fragment in heroic metre, inscribed on a plaque of marble in a pavement surrounding one of the pools and celebrating the famous healing baths.[3] As the most accessible and original of Eudocia's extant works, it is this piece which I have translated here.

Eudocia's poem is erudite, with many direct Homeric echoes, as one might expect of a writer so versed in his work.[4] However, like that of Melinno and Julia Balbilla, her poetry has been criticised for its lack of technical skill, with one commentator finding it 'uncouth and ignorant', and even sympathetic studies deeming

---

[1] Holum, 1982: 169-70; Cameron, 1982: 271-89.
[2] Although Sarah Pomeroy suggests that, in Hellenistic times, fathers passed on musical or scholarly skills to their daughters, in lieu of dowries (1977: 62).
[3] Green & Tsafrir, 1982.
[4] See No.100, notes 8 & 5.

it of historical interest only.[5] Yet the Hammat Gader fragment, like so much of classical women's poetry, displays a grasp of literary artifice, employing such devices as internal rhyme and alliteration. Most of all, it is remarkable for its combination of poetic image and technical language, pagan mythology and Christian worship.[6]

---

[5] Cameron, 1982: 279; Snyder, 1989: 141.

[6] See No.100, notes 9 & 17; Clark, 1994: 137.

[7] **Augusta**: Eudocia had been given the title by Theodosius in AD 423, after the birth of her daughter, Licinia Eudocia.

[8] These lines echo the *Iliad* 2.488-89.

[9] **noble spa**: Eudocia uses the Greek word *klibanus*, which usually referred to the furnace, and meant literally 'oven', in the specific sense of the part of the bath where the natural hot springs were tempered with cold (see Green & Tsafrir, 1989: 85).

[10] **physician**: An annual festival of healing was held at Hammat Gader, for both Christians and pagans.

[11] **four-fold four**: An echo of Homer's description of Calypso's cave in the *Odyssey* 5.70-1.

[12] **name you now**: Eudocia proceeds to list the various rooms and complexes of the Baths.

[13] **India, Matrona**: The meaning of these names is obscure, but they could refer to two rooms decorated with Indian women and 'matrons' (see Green & Tsafrir: 87).

[14] **Repentius**: Perhaps a donor after whom one of the rooms had been named (see Green & Tsafrir).

[15] **Antoninus**: Possibly a reference to the emperor, Antoninus Pius (AD 137-61), who might have been an earlier benefactor of the baths (see Green & Tsafrir).

100: The Baths at Hammat Gader

by Eudocia Augusta [7]

Countless marvels have I seen in life, endless wonders,
but even with a thousand tongues, who could tell your fame,[8]
noble spa,[9] too great to grasp by mere mortals.
                                                So let
me name you for a fiery ocean, newly turning –
physician,[10] parent, the provider of such sweet streams.
From you is born this never-ending swell, rushing here
and then there, now white-hot, now wintry, now warm to touch,
your beauty pours forth as one from fountains, four fold four.[11]

I name you now: [12] India, Matrona,[13] Repentius,[14]
Elijah the holy prophet, and Antoninus [15]
the Good, dew-drenched Galatea, Hygiea herself,[16]
the large warming baths, and the small,[17] the pearl white waters,
and the old spa-head, long-disused; India again,
Matrona, Briara,[18] the Patriarch,[19] and the Nun: [20]
for those in suffering your strength is constant comfort.
But I sing in praise of God, whose wisdom is far-famed...

---

[16] **Galatea, Hygiea**: A sea-nymph and the goddess of health. Green & Tsafrir note the mingling of Christian and pagan references in this list.

[17] **large warming baths...**: Again, Eudocia uses an apparently technical expression, *chliara*, from the Greek *chliaros* or 'luke-warm', also found on another inscription at the bath-house (see Green & Tsafrir: 89).

[18] **Briara**: An obscure name, although it could be a feminine form of the adjective *briaros*, or 'strong', to agree with 'the Nun' (see Green & Tsafrir: 90).

[19] **the Patriarch**: Probably of Jerusalem.

[20] **the Nun**: Green & Tsafrir suggest this could be a reference to Eudocia herself, although there is no evidence of her having taken a formal vow of celibacy (Green & Tsafrir: 91).

ANONYMOUS

Dedicating a section to anonymous writers in a collection of gender-determined poetry might at first appear perverse. Yet although they have no named author, the poems contained here can all be identified, either through usage or content, sometimes even by linguistic indicators, with the body of women's literature in the classical world.

The poems fall into two categories: inscriptions found on stone or material artefacts, and songs quoted by later writers of miscellanies, like Plutarch in the first or second century AD and Athenaeus in the third. Of these, inscriptions are perhaps the most problematic. As Erinna's two epitaphs for Baucis reveal,[1] the 'I' of the sepulchral poem might not necessarily be that of the author, and, as in Nossis' lament for Rhinthon,[2] may well involve a transference of gender. But the poems included here are all generally accepted, or clearly appear to be, by women. In No. 101, for example, ostensibly a grave-stone written by a woman for her dead friend, Biote is described as Euthylla's *hetaira*, a term which implies sexual intimacy, although most usually between a man and his female or male lover. This rare use to indicate love between women, as well as the absence of any definition of the deceased by her relationship to men – as daughter or wife – suggests (although can never prove) a female authorship. If so, it is of great interest, as one of the very few examples of women's writing from fifth-century Athens, a time when the city was experiencing its great explosion of male literature.[3]

The poems found in quotation raise less complex issues of authorship. All are songs, identified by the writers who cite them as sung specifically by women, either over their domestic chores like No.115,[4] at religious festivals like Nos.111-13, or in their childhood games like No.117.[5] Again, while authorship of any folk literature can only be conjectural, the songs present a valuable glimpse into the everyday lives of ordinary women. And if their names have been lost, unlike those of the more aristocratic women poets, then the words they once sang over and over, at work, play, or prayer, have, at least, been preserved.

---

[1] No.45.
[2] No.80 (see Balmer, 1992: 14).
[3] See Introduction p.10 & Hedyle p.80 & No.71.
[4] See also No.35.
[5] See also No.42, note 16.

Epitaphs

101: Biote[6]

Your love, Biote, was like honey, like truth,
and now I'm placing a slab above your grave.
Set it in stone: Euthylla took you for her
lover[7] and these tears are your memorial
                falling one by one
                      for the years we have lost.

102: Bitte[8]

marble not flesh, a woman turned to stone;
O Bitte, it's all I have left of you –
the memory of your face
                a mother's hardening grief.[9]

103: Phanocrite[10]

Her grieving mother raised this tablet
for Phanocrite,
           a life lost in death:
Farewell, take comfort, my darling girl.

---

[6] From Athens, late fifth century BC.

[7] **lover**: *hetaira* (see p.118).

[8] From Amorgos, mid-fifth century BC.

[9] **a mother's...grief**: The mother's name was usually omitted in early epitaphs, although conventionally only a father's grief would be thought worthy of mention (see Anyte No.50, note 19).

[10] From Erythrae, late sixth century BC. Friedländer & Hoffleit note how the expected 'father' in line 1 is replaced by 'mother' (1948: No.63).

104: A Loyal Daughter [11]

My daughter I raised in Athens, sent her
to serve a foreign Queen; even at court [12]
she still shone, was treasured like a jewel.
And now I have brought her back in a box,
showered her not with golden desert sand
but the warm soft soil of her own homeland.

105: Nausimachus [13]

Beneath this slab sleeps Nausimachus
               his mother laid him down, with love. [14]

106: Gallo [15]

  Gallo's tomb:
His sister set him here
his nurse, his comfort
through the sickness. [16]

---

[11] From Cape Zoster near Athens, mid first century BC.

[12] **Queen...court**: Cleopatra, at the royal court of Alexandria (see Lefkowitz & Fant, 1982: 30).

[13] From the Wall of Themistocles, Athens.

[14] **laid him down**: The Greek verb here, *katthemen*, means 'to set up a memorial' but also has a more general sense 'to set down' or 'lay aside', an echo of the modern expression for putting babies in their cots to sleep.

[15] From Attica, on a marble disc with a spiral inscription, and in a dactylic metre.

[16] **nurse...sickness**: The verb *noseleuein* means specifically 'to tend a sick person through illness' (see Lefkowitz & Fant, 1982, No.54, an inscription to a 'professional' nurse & Pomeroy, 1977: 58-60).

107: Temple Cloak [17]

Praxidice created me, Dyseris drew up my plans;
in this one cloth, the skill of both is stitched.

108: A Prize Vase [18]

For Melosa the conqueror
                    women's champion at carding wool.

109: Melinna's Sacrifice [19]

With the skill of her hands and the courage in her soul,
Melinna raised her family, and this stone to you,
lady Athena, the workers' friend [20] – a share of all
she has sacrificed: a monument to kindness, grace.

---

[17] Stitched into a garment dedicated in an unknown temple, Thessaly, *c.*
fifth century BC. The second line is an elegiac pentameter
[18] An inscription on a black-figure vase, fifth century BC. Such inscriptions
were usually made by the victors themselves.
[19] On an arch in Athens, dated to after 350 BC. For the name Melinna (or
Melinno), see Nos.77 & 84.
[20] **Athena...worker's friend**: Described in the Greek as 'the worker-god-
dess', Athena was the goddess of spinning and wool-working.

Folk Songs:

110: Lovers at Dawn [21]

What do you do to me? I'm on my knees
and begging, please, don't give the game away:
before my man walks in the door, get out
of bed; he'll wipe the floor with you and me.
Believe me, my love, it's already day –
first light is at my window, can't you see?

---

[21] A women's song about a cheating wife, quoted by Athenaeus (*Scholars at Dinner*, 15.697b) as an example of a 'Locrian song', perhaps a reference to Locri's reputation as a city where women were honoured (see p.84 & Nossis No.79, note 45).

Festive Songs

111: Sacrificial Song [22]

Let us go to Athens

[home again]

112: Hymn [23]

Come, Lord Dionysus, come,
to the temples of Elis,
bring your holy Graces
to the temple.

Rage like the bull [24]
horned and hoofed,

worthy bull,
worthy bull.

---

[22] According to Plutarch, sung by Bottiaean girls during the performance of certain sacrifices, and explained by reference to an ancient myth that the people of Bottia in Thrace were descended from the Athenian youths sent as a tribute to Minos in Crete (*Life of Theseus*: 16.2).

[23] Again quoted by Plutarch (*Greek Questions*, 36), as a hymn sung to Dionysus by the women of Elis.

[24] **Rage like the bull**: Pausanias notes that the festival at Elis was called the *Thuia* or 'rage' (*Description of Greece*, 6.26.1). Dionysus was believed to appear in animal form as a bull.

113: The Festival[25]

We've come to worship mother Demeter – a circle of nine,
all girls of a certain age, all dressed in our holiday best –
dressed in our best, and wearing our finest ivory jewels,
stars sawn from the shining sky,

                              a sight that should be seen.

114: Song for Titus Flamininus[26]

So now let us honour the Trust of Rome[27]
a faith to stand guard on far-shining oaths.

Sing, girls, Sing!
Lift up your voices
to great Zeus and
Roma too[28]

to Titus, the Trust
of Rome.
Praise Him!

Titus, our saviour.

---

[25] This fragment has been attributed to Erinna (see Bowra, 1936: 160).
Demeter was worshipped by women as a mother corn-goddess (see Dorothy
Wellesley's poem, 'Demeter in Spring' [in Bernikow, 1979: 162-64]).

[26] This song was performed at Chalcis in 191 BC. In 194 BC, Titus Quinc-
tius Flamininus had removed the Roman garrison, imposed during the war
with Macedonia, from the city.

[27] **Trust of Rome**: The Greek is a translation of the Latin *Fides Publica*,
the promise of protection in the name of the state.

[28] **Roma**: A Greek goddess personifying Roman power. She also appears
in Melinno's 'Hymn to Roma', No.84.

[29] Another song quoted by Plutarch (*Seven Sages*, 14), where Thales, one
of the wise men assembled for a fictional dinner-party, remarks that at Eresus
he heard his hostess singing this song as she worked at her handmill (see p.49).

115: Work Song [29]

Grind, mill, grind!

as the tyrant once ground
      great cities, many oats. [30]

116: The Scorpion [31]

A scorpion waits under every stone:
      take care in case it should suddenly strike –
deceit creeps in with the dark
              and the unknown.

117: Girls' Game [32]

Mrs Tortoise, Mrs Tortoise, what are doing in the round?
      I'm spinning this fine black thread into a fine black shroud.

Mrs Tortoise, Mrs Tortoise, how did your child come to die?
      He leapt from white, white horses between the waves and sky.

---

[30] **tyrant...ground...oats**: In the text the 'tyrant' is Pittacus, ruler of Mytilene in Lesbos during Sappho's lifetime in the sixth century BC. The Greek puns on Pittacus 'grinding' the people and his apparently prolific sexual activity – said to be his daily exercise (Diogenes Laertius, 81; see Campbell, 1993: 253).

[31] Quoted in a list of *skolia* or drinking-songs by Athenaeus (*Scholars at Dinner*, 15.693f-694c). The first line also appears, with a slightly different word-ing, in Aristophanes' play *Thesmophoriazusae* (528), and is attributed by a scholiast on the line to Praxilla (see No.38).

[32] Quoted by Pollux (9.122s), who calls it specifically a girls' game. Bowra later identified it as the game referred to in Erinna's 'Distaff' (1936: 154; see No.42, note 16).

RIDDLES: CLEOBULINA

Riddles might be considered to belong more rightly to the preceding section of anonymous verse, except for their attribution by some of the ancient writers who quote them to a woman, Cleobulina, thought to date from the sixth century BC.[1] According to Plutarch, she was one of the most 'admirable and famous women' of the ancient world,[2] although today only a few semi-mythological stories about her survive. Diogenes Laertius claims she was the daughter of one Cleobulus of Rhodes, a philosopher who also wrote riddles, and believed in the education of women, instructing his daughter in his literary skills. She was also thought to be the mother of Thales, one of the seven wise men of antiquity.[3] Plutarch records that although her riddles were known for their wit and dexterity as far away as Egypt, her real talents were her learning, political judgement and grasp of philosophy.[4]

Such stories, however, may be apocryphal. Ancient commentators record that both Cratinus in the fifth century and Alexis in the fourth to third centuries BC wrote comic plays called 'The Cleobulinas', and it is possible that humorous material from these works was seized on by much later writers in the same way that scurrilous details from comedies about Sappho later became the basis for assumptions about her life.[5]

Whatever the details of Cleobulina's biography, or indeed the questions surrounding her very existence, the stories told about her indicate two interesting points: the emphasis on her great learning, even her grasp of political life, at a time when women were more normally excluded from both, and the celebration of her wit. Throughout the centuries, women's art has not normally been associated with humour; the attribution of such well-loved jokes to Cleobulina in the presence of a male candidate, her 'father' Cleobulus, to whom two other riddles are credited, is doubly surprising. But as Anyte and the two Sulpicias have already shown, a dazzling verbal dexterity was one of the classical women poets' greatest skills – and provides a fitting farewell tribute to their art.

---

[1] Pomeroy, 1975: 56.
[2] *Conjugal Precepts*, 48.
[3] Diogenes Laertius, *Lives of the Philosophers*, 1.89; 1.22.
[4] *Seven Sages*, 3.
[5] See Lefkowitz, 1981b; Balmer, 1992: 11-12.

118: The Cheat

I saw one man cheat another and steal from him by force;
but in this case might was right, so everybody thought.

What did I see?

A man disarming a lunatic.

119: Blood-Brothers

I saw one man welded in bronze to another,
until the two became as one – in blood, brothers.

What did I see?

A physician bleeding a patient into a cupping instrument.[6]

120: The Bones

Alive my braying voice could drive a man to tears;
dead my knobbly bones will bring pleasure to your ears.

What am I?

A flute made from an ass's bone.[7]

---

[6] **cupping-instrument**: A glass cup with an open mouth used in ancient and medieval medicine for bleeding patients. Blood was drawn into the cup, which was purified by heat, by making incisions in the skin (or 'scarifying').

[7] **ass's bone**: Plutarch, who quotes this riddle, notes that flute-makers had abandoned fawns' bones for asses', which were said to improve the sound (*Seven Sages*, 5).

APPENDICES

CLASSICAL WOMEN POETS

Alcinoë, Greek itinerant poet, Thronion, third century BC. No work survives.

Anyte, Greek epigrammatist, Tegea, *c*. 300 BC. Twenty-one surviving epigrams (three more attributed to her but of dubious authorship): Nos.50-70.

Aristodama, Greek itinerant poet, Smyrna, *c*. 220 BC. No work survives.

Aristomache, Greek itinerant epic poet, Erythrae, before 200 BC. No work survives.

Charixena, Greek lyric poet, Athens? fifth century BC? No work survives.

Cleobulina, Greek poet and composer of riddles, *c*. sixth century BC? Three riddles attributed in ancient sources: Nos. 118-20.

Corinna, Greek poet, Tanagra, *c*. fifth or third century B.C? About forty fragments survive: Nos.9-34.

Diophila, Greek astronomer poet, Alexandria, *c*. 300 BC. No work survives.

Erinna, Greek poet, Tenos? *c*. 350 BC. Six poems and fragments survive: Nos.42-46.

Eudocia, Greek Christian poet, Byzantium/Jerusalem, *c*. AD 400-460. Epic Christian verses and a papyrus fragment survive: No.100.

Glauce, Greek poet, Chios, date uncertain. No work survives.

Hedyle, Greek poet, Athens, third century BC. One fragment survives: No.71.

Julia Balbilla, Greek poet, Rome, *c*. AD 130. Four graffitied poems survive: Nos.94-97.

Melinno, Greek poet, second century BC or second century AD? One hymn survives: No.84.

Moero, Greek epic poet and epigrammatist, Byzantium, *c*. 300 BC. Three poems survive: Nos.47-49.

Moschine, Greek poet, Athens, *c.* 325 BC, mother of Hedyle. No work survives.

Myrtis, Greek lyric poet, Anthedon, fifth century BC. No work survives.

Nicobule, Greek poet, date and origins uncertain. No work survives.

Nossis, Greek epigrammatist, Locri, *c.* 300 BC. Twelve epigrams survive: Nos.72-83.

Parthenis, Greek epigrammatist, before 100 BC. No work survives.

Perilla, Latin poet, Rome, late first century BC. No work survives.

Praxilla, Greek poet, Sicyon, mid-fifth century BC. Six fragments survive: Nos.38-41.

Proba, Latin poet, Rome, fourth century AD. A Virgilian cento survives: Nos.98-99.

Salpe, Greek poet, wrote a work called 'The Sports', date and origins uncertain. No work survives.

Sappho, Greek lyric poet, Lesbos, sixth century BC. Over two hundred extant fragments: Nos.1-8.

Sempronia, Latin poet, Rome, first century BC. No work survives.

Sulpicia, Latin elegiac poet, Rome, late first century BC. Six or eight fragments survive: Nos.85-92.

Sulpicia (II), Latin satirical poet, Rome, first century AD. Two lines survive: No.93.

Telesilla, Greek poet, Argos, early fifth century BC. Five fragments survive: Nos.35-37.

ANCIENT WRITERS AND SOURCES MENTIONED IN THE TEXT [1]

Aelian, Greek rhetorician and writer of miscellanies, *c.* AD 170-235.

Aeschylus, Greek tragedian, 525/456 BC.

Aesop, Greek fable-teller, early sixth century BC.

Alcaeus, Greek lyric poet, *c.* 620 - *c.* 580 BC.

Alexis, Greek comic playwright *c.* 375 - *c.* 275 BC.

Anacreon, Greek lyric poet, *c.* 570-485 BC.

Antipater of Thessalonica, Greek epigrammatist, *fl. c.* 10 BC-AD 20.

Antiphanes, Greek comic playwright, *fl.* 385 BC

A.P. (*Anthologia Palatina*). See Palatine Anthology.

Apollodorus, Greek mythographer, first or second century AD.

Apollonius Dyscolus, Greek grammarian, second century AD.

Archilochus, Greek iambic and elegiac poet, *c.* 680-640 BC.

Aristophanes, Greek comic playwright *c.* 450-385 BC.

Asclepiades, Greek epigrammatist, *fl.* 290 BC.

Athenaeus, Greek writer and anthologist, *fl. c.* AD 200.

Ausonius, Latin (and Greek) poet, *d.c.* AD 395.

Callimachus, Greek poet, *c.* 305-240 BC.

Catullus, Latin poet, *c.* 85-54 BC.

Cicero, Roman orator and philosopher, 106-43 BC.

Cratinus, Greek comic playwright, *fl. c.* 450-421 BC.

Diogenes Laertius, Greek biographer, early third century AD.

Euripides, Greek tragedian, *c.* 485-406 BC.

Eusebius, Greek/Latin Christian chronicler, *c.* 260-340 BC.

Hephaestion, Greek metrician, AD 130-169.

Herodas, Greek mime-writer, third century BC.

---

[1] In this listing, 'Greek' or 'Latin' refers to the language works were written in, and not necessarily to the subject's place of origin.

Herodotus, Greek historian, fifth century BC.

Hesiod, Greek epic poet, *c*. 700 BC.

Hesychius, Greek lexicographer, fifth century AD.

Homer, name given by Greeks to author of the epic poems, the *Iliad* and the *Odyssey*.

Iliad, Greek epic poem on the war between Greece and Troy, attributed by the ancients to Homer, probably composed in the eighth century BC, and reached a final, written form *c*. 700 BC.

Isidore of Seville, Latin Christian scholar, *c*. AD 602-36.

Jerome, Latin Christian writer and scholar, AD 348-420.

Julianus, Greek epigrammatist, fifth century AD.

Juvenal, Latin satirist, *fl. c*. AD 100-118.

Leonidas, Greek epigrammatist, *c*. 300 BC.

Lysias, Greek orator, *c*. 459-*c*. 380 BC.

Malalas, Johannes, Greek rhetorician and historian, *c*. AD 491-578.

Marcus Argent, Greek epigrammatist, *fl*. early first century BC/AD.

Martial, Latin satirist, *c*. AD 40 - *c*. 104.

Maximus of Tyre, Greek philosopher and rhetorician, *c*. AD 125-185.

Meleager, Greek epigrammatist and anthologist, *fl*. 100 BC.

Mnasalces, Greek epigrammatist, *fl. c*. 250 BC.

New Comedy, a genre of Greek comic plays based around domestic melodramas, and performed at Athens in the late fourth century BC.

Nicander, Greek poet, second century BC.

Niceratus, Greek sculptor, *fl. c*. 100 BC.

Odyssey, Greek epic poem, attributed to Homer, recounting the ten-year wanderings of Odysseus on his way home to Ithaca after the Trojan War.

Oppian, Greek poet, late second century AD.

Orosius, Latin Christian chronicler, *fl*. AD 415.

Ovid, Latin poet, 43 BC – AD 17.

Palatine Anthology, compiled from earlier Greek epigrams, *c*. AD 980.

Pausanias, Greek traveller and geographer, *fl. c.* AD 150.

Pindar, Greek choral poet, 518-438 BC.

Plato, Greek philosopher, *c*. 429-347 BC.

Plautus, Latin comic playwright, second century BC.

Plutarch, Greek biographer, moralist and essayist, first century AD.

Pollux, Greek lexicographer and rhetorician, second century AD.

Polybius, Greek historian, *c*. 200 – *c*. 118 BC.

Propertius, Latin elegiac poet, second half of first century BC.

Rhinthon, Greek burlesque writer, early third century BC.

Scholiast, an ancient textual commentary, often anonymous.

Sidonius Apollinaris, Latin poet, AD 430 – *c*. 479.

Silanion, Greek sculptor, fourth century BC.

Sophocles, Greek tragedian, *c*. 496 BC – 406 BC.

Stobaeus, Greek anthologist, early fifth century AD.

Strabo, Greek geographer, 64/63 BC – AD 21.

Suda, a Greek lexicon, compiled in the tenth century AD.

Tatian, Greek Christian writer, mid-second century AD.

Terence, Latin comic playwright, *c*. 190 -159 BC.

Theocritus, Greek pastoral poet, *c*. 300 -260 BC.

Theodosius, Greek grammarian, *fl. c.* AD 400.

Theognis, Greek elegiac poet, *c*. 550-480 BC.

Tibullus, Latin elegiac poet, *c*. 55-19 BC.

Timotheus, Greek poet, *c*. 450 -360 BC.

Tyrtaeus, Greek elegiac poet, mid-seventh century BC.

Xenophon, Greek historian, *c*. 428/7 – *c*. 354 BC.

Zenobius, Greek rhetorician, second century AD.

GLOSSARY

Acheron, a river of the Underworld, the kingdom of the dead. See Anyte No.50.

Achilles, one of the Greek commanders at Troy, and a hero of the *Iliad*. After an argument with the Greek commander, Agamemnon, over the slave-girl, Briseis, he refused to fight. His friend, Patroclus, took his place and was killed by Hector, son of Priam, the king of Troy. In revenge, Achilles then killed Hector. See Praxilla No.40.

Acraephen, a mythological prophet, one of the fifty sons of the giant hunter, Orion. See Corinna No.11.

Adelphius, husband of Proba, prefect of Rome in AD 351.

Admetus, mythological king of Pherae in Thessaly. Apollo promised he could live forever if someone else would die in his place; only his wife, Alcestis, offered but was rescued from Hades by the hero, Heracles. See Praxilla No.41(I).

Adonia, annual Greek women's festival dedicated to worship of Adonis, celebrated with wine and laughter. See Praxilla No.39.

Adonis, women's fertility god, lover of Aphrodite. See Praxilla No.39 & Nossis No.78.

Aegean, sea between Greece and Asia Minor.

Aeneas, Trojan hero, founder of Rome in Virgil's eponymous epic, the *Aeneid*.

Agamemnon, king of Mycenae, husband of Clytemnestra, who later murdered him, and leader of Greek troops at Troy.

Ajax, king of Salamis, brother of Teucer and one of the Greek heroes at Troy, where he stabbed and killed himself in a battle-rage.

Alcyone, a daughter of Poseidon, threw herself into the sea when her lover, Ceyx, was drowned, and was transformed into a kingfisher. See Hedyle No.71.

Alexandria, Egyptian city at the head of the Nile delta, famous for its libraries.

Alpheus, a river in the Peloponnese. Its river-god pursued the goddess Artemis, or, in some versions, the nymph, Arethusa. See Telesilla No.35.

Amenoth, or Amenhotep III, deified Egyptian king, whose temple housed the colossi of Memnon. See Julia Balbilla No.95.

Amorgos, small island in the Aegean sea.

Amphion, a Boeotian hero, the son of Zeus by Antiope. He was the inventor of music, said to have raised the walls of Thebes with his songs.

Andromache, wife of Hector, prince of Troy.

Anthedon, city in Boeotia, home of Myrtis.

Antinous, a beautiful youth loved by the emperor Hadrian, he drowned in the Nile in AD 130.

Antioch, city in Syria.

Antiochus IV, King of Commagene, a district of Syria, AD 38-72, grandfather to Julia Balbilla. See No.95.

Antiope, daughter of Nycteus, king of Thebes and mother, by Zeus, of the hero Amphion. See Corinna No.21.

Antoninus Pius, Roman emperor, AD 137-61, known for his integrity. See Eudocia No.100.

Aphrodite, the Greek goddess of love, often invoked in classical women's poetry. See Nossis Nos.73, 76 & 78.

Apis, Egyptian god, worshipped in the form of an ox. See Julia Balbilla No.95.

Apollo, son of Leto and Zeus, brother of Artemis, the Greek god of music, medicine and prophecy, as well as the sun-god. See Telesilla No.36.

Arcadia, a mountainous region of the Greek Peloponnese, home of Anyte and characterised as a pastoral paradise in later poetry.

Ares, god of war.

Arete, in the *Odyssey*, Queen of Phaeacia, and mother of Nausicaa.

Arethusa, in Ovid's *Metamorphoses*, a sea-nymph pursued by the river-god Alpheus, and changed by Artemis into a fountain to evade him. See Telesilla No.35.

Argos, city in the Peloponnese, home of Telesilla.

Arno, a river in Etruria near Rome. See Sulpicia No.86.

Artemis, daughter of Leto and Zeus, sister of Apollo, a virgin huntress, also goddess of childbirth, and like Aphrodite often invoked in classical women's poetry. See Sappho No.8, Telesilla No.35, Nossis No.82.

Asopus, a river of Boeotia and its god. See Corinna No.11.

Athena, daughter of Zeus, a warrior goddess of wisdom, and of spinning. See Anyte No.69 & Anonymous. No.109.

Attica, a region of Greece, with Athens as its most famous city.

Atlas, giant who held up the world on his shoulders.

Balbillus, Tiberius Claudius, ancestor of Julia Balbilla, astronomer and prefect of Egypt, AD 55-59. See Julia Balbilla No.95.

Boeotia, district of Greece to the north of Athens, home to Pindar, Myrtis and Corinna.

Boeotus, founding hero of Boeotia, son of Melanippe and Poseidon. See Corinna No.31.

Bottiaea, a region of Macedonia. See Anonymous No. 111.

Briseis, in the *Iliad*, a captive of the Greeks, fought over by Achilles and Agamemnon.

Byzantium, city on Bosphorus, capital of eastern Roman empire.

Cadmus, founder of Thebes. After killing a dragon, he sowed its teeth, and almost immediately a crop of fully-armed men sprang from the ground, the *Spartoi*, or sown men, who helped him build the city. See Melinno No.84.

Calenus, in Martial's *Satires*, the husband of Sulpicia the satirist; his name also appears in her only fragment. See No.93.

Cambyses, Persian king who conquered Egypt in 525 BC, and was said to have sacked the colossi of Memnon. See Julia Balbilla No.95.

Cassiopeia, Queen of Ethiopia, mother of Andromeda and the nymph, Libya. She was later set in the stars as a constellation. See Corinna No.9.

Castalian font, a spring on Mount Parnassus, sacred to the Muses, whose waters were said to confer poetic powers. See Proba No.98.

Cephisus, a local Boeotian river-god and founder of Tanagra, Corinna's city. See Corinna No.9

Ceres, Roman corn-goddess, associated with Demeter.

Chalcis, a Greek city in Euboea. See Anonymous No.114.

Chios, large island off the coast of Asia Minor.

Circe, a mythical enchantress, who falls in love with Glaucus and transforms her rival, Scylla, into a sea-monster. See Hedyle No.71.

Cithaeron, mountain in Boeotia, sacred to the Muses. See Corinna No. 10.

Cleitor, a town to the north of Arcadia. See Anyte No.69.

Cleon, populist Athenian politician and general in the fifth century BC, butt of Aristophanes' jokes. See Praxilla No.41(I).

Cleopatra, Queen of Egypt, 51-30 BC See Anonymous No.104.

Clytemnestra, sister of Helen and Queen of Mycenae. Her husband, Agamemnon, sacrificed their daughter Iphigenia to appease the gods on the way to Troy; on his return she murdered him, only to be killed in turn by their son, Orestes.

Constantius II, emperor of Rome, AD 324-361.

Coryphum, a mountain in Epidaurus, sacred to Artemis. See Telesilla No.35.

Cronus, the son of Uranus and Gaia (Heaven and Earth) and father of Zeus. See Corinna 10 & Moero No.47.

Croton, a Greek town in southern Italy.

Curetes, guardians of Zeus during his childhood on Crete, they warned off unwelcome visitors with their clashing cymbals. See Corinna No.10 & Moero No.47.

Cycnus, son of Hyrie, a mythological heroine of Boeotia; when he died, she wept so much that she was turned into a fountain. See Corinna No.24.

Cypris, a title of Aphrodite, said to have sprung from the foam of the sea at Paphos in Cyprus. See Nossis No.72.

Daedalus, mythological Greek craftsman, who built the maze on Crete for Minos.

Daphnephoria, a festival to Apollo, celebrated every ninth year at Thebes in Boeotia. See Corinna No.12.

Delos, an island in the Cyclades in the Aegean Sea, birthplace of

Apollo and Artemis. See Nossis No.82.

Demeter, the goddess of corn and harvest, also known as Ceres. Her sanctuary at Eleusis in Attica was the centre of her worship. See Melinno No.84 & Anonymous No.113.

Diana, Roman goddess of the hunt and chastity, associated with Artemis. See Sulpicia No.92.

Dido, mythological Queen of Carthage, committed suicide when deserted by her lover, Aeneas.

Dionysus, god of wine, fertility and poetic inspiration. See Anonymous No.112.

Domitian, tyrannical emperor of Rome, AD 81-96, exiled philosophers from Rome and persecuted Christians.

Elis, a region and city in the Greek Peloponnese. See Anonymous No.112.

Endymion, a shepherd, lover of Selene, the moon, or in some versions, Artemis as moon-goddess.

Eös, the dawn, lover of the mortal, Tithonus. See Julia Balbilla No.95.

Epidaurus, city in the north-west of Argos on the Greek Peloponnese.

Eresus, a town on Lesbos. See Anonymous No.115.

Eros, playful god of sexual desire, the attendant of Aphrodite.

Erythrae, Greek city on the Ionian coast of Asia Minor, opposite the island of Chios.

Erythraean Sea, or 'Red Sea', the Indian Ocean. See Hedyle No.71.

Eteocles, King of Thebes, fought over the city with his brother Polyneices after the death of their father, Oedipus. See Corinna No.32.

Etna, a volcano on Sicily, whose eruptions were known to the Greeks at least from the time of Pindar. See Hedyle No.71.

Euboea, large island in the Aegean Sea, just off the mainland.

Eunostus, a hero of Tanagra. The story of his cousin Ochna's tragic love for him was told in a lost poem by Myrtis of Anthedon.

Euonymus, a Boeotian river-god and prophet. See Corinna No.11.

Euripus, a narrow strait which separated Euboea from Boeotia.

Evander, a mythical Greek king who in the *Aeneid*, had settled the site of Rome, but helped Aeneas fight the Italians for the land.

Flamininus, Titus Quinctius, a Roman general in the wars between Rome and Philip of Macedon, 198-196 BC. See Anonymous No.114.

Galatea, a sea-nymph, loved by the Cyclops Polyphemus. See Eudocia No.100.

Ganymede, a beautiful youth loved by Zeus. See Corinna No.33.

Glaucus, a son of Poseidon who was transformed into a sea-god or, according to Ovid, a merman. See Hedyle No.71.

Graces, companions of Aphrodite, three goddesses of beauty and charm. See Nossis No.82.

Hades, the name for both the Underworld, or realm of the dead, and the God who rules it. See Erinna No.43.

Hadrian, Roman emperor, AD 117-138. Julia Balbilla accompanied his wife Sabina on a trip to Egypt in AD 130. See Nos.94-97.

Hector, prince of Troy, Andromache's husband, and son of Priam, who was killed by Achilles in the Trojan War. Andromache's lament over his body is one of the most moving scenes in the *Iliad*.

Helen, wife of Menelaus of Sparta, famous for her beauty, whose elopement to Troy with Paris provoked the ten-year war between Greece and Troy, subject of Homer's *Iliad*. See Sappho No.4.

Helicon, mountain in Boeotia, sacred to the Muses. See Corinna No.10.

Hera, goddess of hearth and home, unhappily married to Zeus. See Telesilla No.37 & Nossis No.79.

Heracles, mythological Greek hero, rescued Alcestis from Hades, known in Roman mythology as Hercules.

Hermes, son of Zeus and Maia, messenger of the gods. See Corinna Nos. 10 & 11.

Hesperus, the evening star. See Sappho No.7.

Hippasos, nephew of the daughters of Minyas, he was torn to pieces by his aunts in their Bacchic trance. See Corinna No.23.

Hymen, God of marriage. See Erinna No.45 (I).

Hygiea, ancient goddess of health. See Eudocia No.100.

Hyria, an area of Boeotia, with a town of the same name, founded by the nymph Hyrie. See Corinna No.21.

Hyrie, founding heroine of Hyria, at the death of her son, Cycnus, she wept so much she was turned into a fountain. See Corinna No.24.

Hyrieus, son of Poseidon and Alcyone, father of Orion. See Corinna No.11.

Inopus, a river on the island of Delos, sacred to Artemis. See Nossis No.82.

Iolaus, a hero of Boeotia, and companion of Heracles; lovers swore eternal fidelity on his shrine. The title of a poem by Corinna. See No.13.

Jocasta, Oedipus' wife – and mother, who committed suicide when she realised the truth.

Jove, Roman version of Zeus.

Julian, Roman emperor, AD 360-363, bought up a Christian but converted to paganism and attempted to revive pagan worship throughout the empire.

Lacinium, a promontory near Croton in southern Italy, which housed a shrine to Hera, sometimes known as 'Lacinia' after it. See Nossis No.79.

Ladon, a river in Boeotia. See Corinna No.29.

Leontius, late fourth to early fifth century AD, Athenian sophist, father of Eudocia.

Lesbos, island off the coast of Asia Minor, home to Sappho.

Leto, mother of Apollo and Artemis. See Corinna No.11 & Nossis No.82.

Libya, a nymph, daughter of Cassiopeia. See Corinna No.9.

Locri, a Greek town in southern Italy, home of Nossis. See Anyte No.61, Nossis Nos.81 & 83 and Anonymous No.110.

Lydia, a country in Asia Minor, renowned for its wealth and power. See Sappho Nos.3 & 4.

Macedonia, a country bordering Greece to the north east.

Magnentius, usurper to the Roman empire, defeated by Constantius II at the battle of Mursa in AD 351 and later committed suicide.

Maia, a daughter of Atlas and Pleione, the mother of Hermes by Zeus, and one of the seven Pleiades. See Corinna No.11.

Melanippe, mother of Boeotus.

Memnon, a mythical King of Egypt who helped Priam defend Troy, but was killed by the Greeks. His vast statue, or colossi, at Thebes on the Nile, was said to 'sing' at dawn – a greeting to his mother, Eös. See Julia Balbilla Nos.94–97.

Menelaus, mythical king of Sparta, cuckolded husband of Helen. See Sappho No.4.

Menippe, a daughter of Orion and heroine of Boeotia. See Corinna No.20.

Merope, daughter of King Oenopion, loved by the hunter, Orion. See Corinna No.30.

Messalla, M. Valerius Corvinus, 64 BC - AD 8, a literary patron in Rome, and probably Sulpicia's uncle and guardian. See Sulpicia No.86.

Metioche, a daughter of Orion, sister of Menippe, and a heroine of Boeotia. See Corinna No.20.

Minos, mythical King of Crete, he commissioned Daedalus to build a maze to house the monstrous Minotaur, the product of his wife Pasiphaë's passion for a bull.

Minyas, mythical king of Boeotia. See Corinna No.23.

Mormo, a monstrous female in ancient Greek folklore. See Erinna No.42.

Muses, nine goddesses of literature, music and dance, connected with poetic inspiration. See Corinna Nos.9-10, 14-16, 27; Nossis Nos.80 & 83; Proba No.98.

Mytilene, leading city of the island of Lesbos, home of Sappho. See Nossis No.83.

Nero, Roman emperor AD 54-68.

Nycteus, king of Thebes, father of Antiope.

Oedipus, king of Thebes, husband and son of Jocasta, father and brother of Eteocles and Polyneices.

Oenopion, King of Chios, father of Orion's lover, Merope. See Corinna No.30.

Ochna, see Eunostus.

Ogygus, mythical king of Boeotia. See Corinna No.31(II).

Olympus, mountain in Thessaly, home of the Greek gods.

Orestes, son of Clytemnestra and Agamemnon, rulers of Mycenae. When Clytemnestra murdered Agamemnon, Orestes killed her in revenge.

Orion, giant hero of Boeotia, after his death, set in the stars. See Corinna Nos.9, 11, 30.

Ortygia, island near Delos where Artemis was born. See Nossis No.82.

Palinurus, in the *Aeneid*, the helmsman of Aeneas' ship. See Proba No.99.

Pallas, in the *Aeneid*, the son of Evander, killed by Turnus in the battle for the site of Rome.

Pan, a rural god of Arcadia, represented as a part-goat herdsman, playing the pipes. See Anyte Nos.56, 60 & 70.

Pandarus, daughters of, Aido and Chelidone. When Aido's husband, Polytechnus, raped Chelidone, the sisters murdered Aido's son, Itys, and served his flesh to his unwitting father. They were later transformed into a nightingale and swallow.

Paris, prince of Troy, lover of Helen.

Parnassus, a mountain north of Delphi, sacred to the Muses and Apollo.

Patroclus, Greek hero at Troy, friend of Achilles, and killed by Hector.

Penelope, in the *Odyssey*, Queen of Ithaca and the faithful wife of Odysseus.

Penthesilea, Amazon queen, daughter of Ares, who fought for Troy against the Greeks. See Melinno No.84.

Pentheus, a mythical king of Thebes, who mocked the worship of Dionysus or Bacchus, and was torn to pieces by his mother, Agave, in punishment, during a Bacchic frenzy.

Persephone, daughter of Demeter or Ceres, Queen of the Underworld and wife of Hades.

Pherae, city of Thessaly.

Pittacus, tyrant of Mytilene on Lesbos, *c.* 645-570 BC. See Anonymous No.115.

Pleiades, seven daughters of Atlas, pursued by Orion, who were transformed into a constellation. They were also characterised as doves. See Moero No.47.

Polyneices, prince of Thebes, son of Oedipus and Jocasta, fought a civil war with his brother Eteocles after Oedipus' death. See Corinna No.32.

Poseidon, sea-god, brother of Zeus. See Corinna No.11.

Prometheus, stole fire from the Gods for man, and, in some traditions, created man out of clay, persuading Athena to breathe life into his images. See Erinna No.46.

Pythaeus, a son of Apollo. See Telesilla No.36.

Rhea, mother of Zeus, whom she saved from his murderous father Cronus and hid on Crete. See Corinna No.10 & Moero No.47.

Rhodes, Greek island off coast of Asia Minor.

Roma, Greek goddess personifying the power of Rome. See Melinno No.84.

Sabina, wife of the emperor Hadrian, whom Julia Balbilla accompanied to Egypt in AD 130. See Julia Balbilla Nos.94-97.

Samos, Greek island off the coast of Asia Minor.

Sardis, chief city of Lydia. See Sappho No.3.

Scylla, a nymph, lover of Glaucus, later transformed into a six-headed monster by the enchantress Circe. See Hedyle No.71.

Septimius Severus, Roman emperor, AD 193-211.

Sicyon, city west of Corinth on Greek Peloponnese, home of Praxilla.

Sinis, mythical thief. See Anyte No.62.

Sirens, mythological women who lured sailors to their deaths by their irresistible songs. See Hedyle No.71.

Smyrna, sea-port on the Ionian coast of Asia Minor.

Spartoi, see Cadmus.

Syracuse, city colonised by the Greeks in Sicily, home of Rhinthon the comic playwright. See Nossis No.80.

Tanagra, a nymph, daughter of Asopus and also a city in Boeotia, home of Corinna. See Corinna Nos.9, 22 & 30.

Tegea, city in Arcadia, home of Anyte.

Tenos, Greek island in the Cyclades, possible home of Erinna and Baucis. See Erinna No.45 (II).

Teucer, see Ajax.

Thales, one of the legendary seven wise men of antiquity, reputedly the son of Cleobulina.

Thebes (1), city in Boeotia, founded by Cadmus, later ruled by Oedipus, and home of Pindar. See Corinna Nos. 9,12, 31 & 32.

Thebes (2), city on banks of Nile in Egypt, site of the colossi of Memnon. See Julia Balbilla Nos.94-97.

Theodosius II, Roman emperor, AD 402-450, husband of Eudocia.

Thespeia (or 'Thespia'), a city at the foot of Mount Helicon in Boeotia. See Corinna No.28.

Thessaly, a district of northern Greece.

Thronion, a town in northern Greece.

Tiresias, mythical Greek seer of Thebes.

Titan, god of the sun, which he drove across the sky in his chariot. See Julia Balbilla No.96.

Tithonus, lover of Eös, the dawn, and granted eternal life but not eternal youth, eventually becoming so old and shrivelled that he was transformed into a cicada. See Julia Balbilla No.95.

Venus, goddess of love, Roman equivalent to Aphrodite. See Sulpicia Nos.85 & 91.

Zeus, King of the Gods, son of Cronos and Rhea and husband of Hera. See Corinna No.10 & Moero No.47.

Zoster, a cape and coastal town in Attica near Athens.

TEXTS & ABBREVIATIONS

Bal   Balmer, Josephine, *Sappho: Poems and Fragments* (Newcastle upon Tyne: Bloodaxe Books, 1992).

Bern   Bernand, A.& E., eds, *Les Inscriptions grecques et latines du Colosse de Memnon* (Cairo: Institut français d'archéologie orientale, 1960).

Bow   Bowra, C.M., 'Erinna's *Lament for Baucis*' in *Greek Poetry & Life: Essays Presented to Gilbert Murray* (Oxford: Clarendon Press, 1936), 151-53.

Cam   Campbell, D.A., *Greek Lyric, Vol. I* (London: Loeb Classical Library, 1982).

E   Edmonds, J.M. *Elegy and Iambus* (London: Loeb Classical Library, 1931).

EG   Page, D.L., *Epigrammata Graeca* (Oxford: Clarendon Press, 1975).

FH   Friedländer, P. & Hoffleit, H.B., *Epigrammata: Greek Inscriptions in Verse* (Berkeley: University of California Press, 1948).

Geo   Geoghegan, D., *Anyte: The Epigrams* (Rome: Edizioni dell'Ateneo & Bizzari, 1979).

Gian   Giangrande, G., 'An Epigram of Erinna', *Classical Review*, n.s. 19 (1969), 1-3.

GP   Gow, A.S.F. & Page, D.L., *The Greek Anthology: Hellenistic Epigrams*, 2 vols (Cambridge: Cambridge University Press, 1965).

GT   Green, Judith & Tsafrir, Yoram, 'Greek Inscriptions from Hammat Gader: A Poem by the Empress Eudocia and Two Building Inscriptions', *Israel Exploration Journal*, 32 (1982), 78-91.

Kai   Kaibel, G., *Epigrammata Graeca ex lapidibus conlecta* (Berlin, 1878).

LP   Lobel, E., & Page, D.L., *Poetarum Lesbiorum Fragmenta* (Oxford: Clarendon Press, 1963)

Luck   Luck, George, *Tibullus* (Stuttgart: Teubner, 1988).

PCM   Schenkl, C., ed., *Corpus Scriptorum Ecclesiasticorum Latinorum, Vol. 16: Poetae Christiani Minores* (Vienna: F. Tempsky, 1888).

Pe	**Peek, W.**, *Griechische Vers-Inschriften, I, Grab-epigramme* (Berlin: Akademie-Verlag, 1955).
PMG	**Page, D.L.**, *Poetae Melici Graeci* (Oxford: Clarendon Press, 1962).
Pow	**Powell, J.U.**, ed, *Collectanea Alexandrina* (Oxford: Clarendon Press, 1925).
Rich	**Richlin, Amy**, 'Sulpicia the Satirist', *Classical World*, 86:2 (1992), 125-39.
SEG	*Supplementum Epigraphicum Graecum* (Leiden, 1923).
SH	**Lloyd-Jones, H. & Parsons, P.**, *Supplementum Hellenisticum* (Berlin: Walter de Gruyter, 1983).
West	**West, M.L.**, 'Erinna', in *Zeitschrift für Papyrologie und Epigraphik*, 25 (1977), 95-119.

KEY TO THE POEMS (I)

NO.	TEXT
Sappho:	
1 (I)	LP: 47 (Bal: 1)
1 (II)	LP: 130 (Bal: 2)
1 (III)	LP: i.a.25 (Bal: 5)
2	LP: 31 (Bal: 20)
3	LP: 98 (Bal: 74)
4	LP: 16 (Bal: 21)
5	LP: 112 (Bal: 62)
6	LP: 193 (Bal: 106)
7	LP: 104a (Bal: 110)
8	Cam: 44a (LP 304 Alcaeus)
Corinna:	
9	PMG: 655
10	PMG: 654(i)
11	PMG: 654(ii)
12	PMG: 690
13	PMG: 661
14 (I)	PMG: 692.2a
14 (II)	PMG: 693
15	PMG: 668
16	PMG: 676.a&b
17	PMG: 664(a)
18	PMG: 688
19	PMG: 664(b)
20	PMG: 656
21	PMG: 669
22	PMG: 666
23	PMG: 665
24	PMG: 660
25	PMG: 687;682; 679.a&b;685;683
26	PMG: 678
27	PMG: 677
28	PMG: 674
29	PMG: 684
30 (I)	PMG: 673
30 (II)	PMG: 663;662
31 (I)	PMG: 658
31 (II)	PMG: 671
32	PMG: 659
33	PMG: 680;681;689
34	PMG: 657

NO.	TEXT
Telesilla:	
35	PMG: 723;717; 720
36	PMG: 718;724; 719
37 (I)	PMG: 726(iii)
37 (II)	PMG: 722
Praxilla:	
38	PMG: 750
39	PMG: 747
40	PMG: 748
41 (I)	PMG: 749
41 (II)	PMG: 754
Erinna:	
42	SH: 401
	Bow: 151-53
	West: 112-13
43	SH: 402
44	SH: 404
45 (I)	Gian: 1
45 (II)	GP: 1781
46	GP: 1797
Moero:	
47	Pow: 21
48	GP: 2675
49	GP: 2679
Anyte:	
50	Geo: 5
51	Geo: 8
52	Geo: 6
53	Geo: 7
54	Geo: 16
55	Geo: 18
56	Geo: 19
57	Geo: 17
58	Geo: 15
59	Geo: 14
60	Geo: 13
61	Geo: 10

NO.	TEXT
Anyte *continued*	
62	Geo: 11
63	Geo: 20
64	Geo: 12
65	Geo: 9
66	Geo: 21
67	Geo: 4
68	Geo: 1
69	Geo: 2
70	Geo: 3
Hedyle:	
71	SH: 456
Nossis:	
72	EG: I
73	EG: IV
74	EG: IX
75	EG: VII
76	EG: VI
77	EG: VIII
78	EG: V
79	EG: III
80	EG: X
81	EG: II
82	EG: XII
83	EG: XI
Melinno:	
84	SH: 541
Sulpicia:	
85	Luck: 7 (3.13)
86	Luck: 8 (3.14)
87	Luck: 9 (3.15)
88	Luck: 10 (3.16)
89	Luck: 11 (3.17)
90	Luck: 12 (3.18)
91	Luck: 5 (3.11)
92	Luck: 3 (3.9)
Sulpicia the Satirist:	
93	Rich: 130

NO.	TEXT	NO.	TEXT	NO.	TEXT
Julia Balbilla:		**Anonymous:**		112	PMG: 871
94	Bern: 30	101	Pe: 1415	113	Pow: 186
95	Bern: 29	102	SEG: XV.548	114	Pow: 173
96	Bern: 28	103	FH: 63	115	PMG: 869
97	Bern: 31	104	Kai: 118	116	PMG: 903
		105	FH: 3d	117	PMG: 876(c)
Proba:		106	FH: 161		
98	PCM: 1-23	107	FH: 152	**Riddles ('Cleobulina'):**	
99	PCM: 70-9	108	FH: 177m	118	E: 2
		109	Kai: 776	119	E: 1
Eudocia:		110	PMG: 853	120	E: 3
100	GT: 79	111	PMG: 868		

KEY TO THE POEMS (II)

TEXT	NO.	TEXT	NO.	TEXT	NO.
Bernand:		**E. Graeca** *continued*		**Geoghegan** *continued*	
Bern: 28	96	EG: XI	83	Geo: 16	54
Bern: 29	95	EG: XII	82	Geo: 17	57
Bern: 30	94			Geo: 18	55
Bern: 31	97	**Friedländer**		Geo: 19	56
		& Hoffleit:		Geo: 20	63
Bowra:		FH: 3d	105	Geo: 21	66
Bow: 151-53	42	FH: 63	103		
		FH: 152	107	**Giangrande:**	
Campbell:		FH: 161	106	Gian: 1	45 (I)
Cam: 44a	8	FH: 177m	108		
				Gow & Page:	
Edmonds:		**Geoghegan:**		GP: 1781	45 (II)
E: 1	119	Geo: 1	68	GP: 1797	46
E: 2	118	Geo: 2	69	GP: 2675	48
E: 3	120	Geo: 3	70	GP: 2679	49
		Geo: 4	67		
Epigrammata Graeca:		Geo: 5	50	**Green & Tsafrir:**	
EG: I	72	Geo: 6	52	GT: 79	100
EG: II	81	Geo: 7	53		
EG: III	79	Geo: 8	51	**Kaibel:**	
EG: IV	73	Geo: 9	65	Kai: 8	104
EG: V	78	Geo: 10	61	Kai: 776	109
EG: VI	76	Geo: 11	62		
EG: VII	75	Geo: 12	64	**Lobel & Page:**	
EG: VIII	77	Geo: 13	60	LP: 16	4
EG: IX	74	Geo: 14	59	LP: i.a.25	1 (III)
EG: X	80	Geo: 15	58	LP: 31	2

TEXT	NO.	TEXT	NO.	TEXT	NO.
Lobel & Page *continued*		**P.M. Graeci** *continued*		**P.M. Graeci** *continued*	
LP: 47	1 (I)	PMG: 662	30 (II)	PMG: 726(iii)	37 (I)
LP: 98	3	PMG: 663	30 (II)	PMG: 747	39
LP: 104a	7	PMG: 664(a)	17	PMG: 748	40
LP: 112	5	PMG: 664(b)	19	PMG: 749	41 (I)
LP: 130	1 (ii)	PMG: 665	23	PMG: 750	38
LP: 193	6	PMG: 666	22	PMG: 754	41 (II)
		PMG: 667a&b	16	PMG: 853	110
Luck:		PMG: 668	15	PMG: 868	111
Luck: 3	92	PMG: 669	21	PMG: 869	115
Luck: 5	91	PMG: 671	31 (II)	PMG: 871	112
Luck: 7	85	PMG: 673	30 (I)	PMG: 876(c)	117
Luck: 8	86	PMG: 674	28	PMG: 903	116
Luck: 9	87	PMG: 676a&b	16		
Luck: 10	88	PMG: 677	27	**Powell:**	
Luck: 11	89	PMG: 678	26	Pow: 21	47
Luck: 12	90	PMG: 679a&b	25	Pow: 173	114
		PMG: 680	33	Pow: 186	113
Poetae Christiani		PMG: 681	33		
Minores:		PMG: 682	25	**Richlin:**	
PCM: 1-23	98	PMG: 683	25	Rich: 130	93
PCM: 70-9	99	PMG: 684	29		
		PMG: 685	25	**Supplementum**	
		PMG: 687	25	**Epigraphicum**	
Peek:		PMG: 688	18	**Graecum:**	
Pe: 1415	101	PMG: 689	33	SEG: XV.548	102
		PMG: 690	12		
Poetae Melici Graeci:		PMG: 692(2a)	14 (I)	**Supplementum**	
PMG: 654(i)	10	PMG: 693	14 (II)	**Hellenisticum:**	
PMG: 654(ii)	11	PMG: 717	35	SH: 401	42
PMG: 655	9	PMG: 718	36	SH: 402	43
PMG: 656	20	PMG: 719	36	SH: 404	44
PMG: 657	34	PMG: 720	35	SH: 456	71
PMG: 658	31 (I)	PMG: 722	37 (II)	SH: 541	84
PMG: 659	32	PMG: 723	35		
PMG: 660	24	PMG: 724	36	**West:**	
PMG: 661	13			West: 112-13	42

BIBLIOGRAPHY

Arthur, Marilyn, 'Liberated Women: The Classical Era', in *Becoming Visible: Women in European History*, ed. R. Bridenthal & C. Koonz (Boston: Houghton Mifflin, 1977), 60-89.

Arthur, Marilyn, 'The Tortoise and the Mirror: Erinna PSI 1090', *Classical World*, 74 (1980), 53-65.

Atwood, Margaret, *Poems 1965-75* (London: Virago, 1976).

Baldson, J.P. V.D., *Roman Women* (London: Bodley Head, 1962).

Balmer, Josephine, *Sappho: Poems and Fragments* (Newcastle upon Tyne: Bloodaxe Books, 1992).

Barker, Jonathan, *Thirty Years of the Poetry Book Society: 1956-86* (London: Hutchinson, 1988).

Barnstone, Willis, 'Remembering Sappho,' *Translation Review*, 17 (1985), 9-12.

Barnard, Sylvia, 'Hellenistic Women Poets' *Classical Journal*, 73 (1978), 204-13.

Bassnett, Susan, *Translation Studies*, revised edition (London: Routledge, 1991).

Bernand, A.& E., eds, *Les Inscriptions grecques et latines du Colosse de Memnon* (Cairo: Institut français d'archéologie orientale, 1960).

Bernikow, Louise, *The World Split Open: Women Poets 1552-1950* (London: Women's Press, 1979).

Bogin, Meg, *The Woman Troubadours* (New York, W.W. Norton, 1980).

Boland, Eavan, *Selected Poems* (Manchester: Carcanet, 1989).

Bowman, A.K 'The Roman imperial army: letters and literacy on the northem frontier', in Bowman & Woolf, eds. (1994), 109-25.

Bowman, A.K. & Woolf, G., eds, *Literacy and Power in the Ancient World* (Cambridge: Cambridge University Press, 1994).

Bowra, C.M., 'The Date of Corinna' *Classical Review*, 45 (1931), 4-5.

Bowra, C.M., *Greek Poetry & Life: Essays Presented to Gilbert Murray* (Oxford: Clarendon Press, 1936).

Bowra, C.M., *On Greek Margins* (Oxford: Clarendon Press, 1970).

Braschi, Giannina, *Empire of Dreams*, translated by Tess O'Dwyer (New Haven & London: Yale University Press, 1994).

Brown, Jacqueline, *Thinking Egg* (Todmorden: Littlewood Arc, 1993).

Cameron, A. & A., 'Erinna's Distaff', *Classical Quarterly*, n.s. 19 (1969), 285-88.

Cameron, A., 'The Empress and the Poet: Paganism & Politics at the Court of Theodosius II,' *Yale Classical Studies*, 27 (1982), 271-89.

Campbell, D.A., *Greek Lyric Poetry: A Selection* (London: Macmillan, 1967; reprint, 1976).

Campbell, D.A., *Greek Lyric* (London: Loeb Classical Library, 5 vols, 1982-92).

Cixous, Hélène, 'The Laugh of Medusa', translated by Keith Cohen and Paula Cohen, *Signs*, 1 (Summer 1976), 875-99.

Clark, E.A. & Hatch, D.F., *The Golden Bough, The Oaken Cross: The Virgilian Cento of Faltonia Betitia Proba* (Chicago: Scholars Press, 1981).

Clark, Gillian, *Women in Late Antiquity* (Oxford: Oxford University Press, 1994).

Clayman, Dee Lesser, 'The Meaning of Corinna's Geroia', *Classical Quarterly*, n.s. 28 (1978), 396-97.

Cole, Susan, 'Could Greek Women Read and Write?' in Foley (1981), 219-45.

Cosman, Carol, Keefe, Joan & Weaver, Kathleen, eds., *The Penguin Book of Women Poets* (Harmondsworth: Penguin, 1978).

Costello, Bonnie, 'The "Feminine" Language of Marianne Moore', in McConnell-Ginet, Borker & Furman, eds (1980), 222-38.

DeJean, Joan, 'Fictions of Sappho', *Critical Inquiry*, 13 (1987), 787-805 (Chicago: University of Chicago Press, 1989).

Demand, Nancy, *Thebes in the Fifth Century* (London: Routledge & Kegan Paul, 1982).

Detienne, Marcel, *The Gardens of Adonis: Spices in Greek Mythology* (Brighton: Harvester, 1977).

Devereux, George, 'The Nature of Sappho's Seizure in Fr. 31 LP as Evidence of Her Inversion', *Classical Quarterly* n.s. 20 (1970), 17-31.

Diaz-Diocaretz, Myriam, *Translating Poetic Discourse: Questions of feminist strategies in Adrienne Rich* (Amsterdam: John Benjamin, 1985).

Doolittle, Hilda, *The Collected Poems of H.D.* (New York: Boni & Liveright, 1925).

Dubois, Page, 'Sappho and Helen', *Arethusa*, 11 (1978), 89-99.

Duffy, Carol Ann, *Mean Time* (London: Anvil Press, 1993).

Dunlop, Philip, translator, *The Poems of Tibullus* (Harmondsworth: Penguin, 1972).

Fainlight, Ruth, *This Time of Year* (London: Sinclair-Stevenson, 1994).

Finley, M.I., 'The Silent Women of Rome' in *Aspects of Antiquity* (London: Chatto & Windus, 1968), 129-42.

Foley, H.P., ed., *Reflections of Women in Antiquity*, New York: Gordon & Breach, 1981).

Forché, Carolyn, *The Country Between Us* (London: Jonathan Cape, 1983).

France, Linda, ed., *Sixty Women Poets* (Newcastle upon Tyne: Bloodaxe Books, 1993).

Geoghegan, D., *Anyte: The Epigrams* (Rome: Edizioni dell'Ateneo & Bizzarri, 1979).

Giangrande, G., 'An Epigram of Erinna', *Classical Review*, n.s. 19 (1969), 1-3.

Godard, Barbara, 'Theorizing Feminist Discourse / Translation' in Bassnett, Susan Lefevere, André, eds, *Translation, History and Culture* (London: Pinter, 1990), 89-96.

Gow, A.S.F. & Page, D.L., *The Greek Anthology: Hellenistic Epigrams*, 2 vols (Cambridge: Cambridge University Press, 1965).

Green, Judith & Tsafrir, Yoram, 'Greek Inscriptions from Hammat Gader: A Poem by the Empress Eudocia and Two Building Inscriptions', *Israel Exploration Journal*, 32 (1982), 78-91.

Greer, Germaine, *Kissing the Rod: An Anthology of Seventeenth-Century Women's Verse* (London: Virago, 1988).

Greer, Germaine, 'A Biodegradable Art: Changing Fashions in Anthologies of Women's Poetry', *Times Literary Supplement* (30 June 1995), 78.

Gruppe, O.F., *Die römische Elegie* (Leipzig: 1838).

Hallet, Judith, 'Sappho and Her Social Context: Sense and Sensuality,' *Signs*, 4 (1979), 447-64.

Hallet, Judith, 'Feminist Theory, Historical Periods', in Rabinowitz Richlin, eds (1993), 44-72.

Hallet, Judith, 'Martial's Sulpicia and Propertius' Cynthia', in DeForest, Mary, ed., *Essays in Honour of Joy King* (Chicago: Bolchazy-Carducci, 1993), 322-53.

Hammond, N.G.L. & Scullard, H.H., eds, *The Oxford Classical Dictionary*, 2nd edition (Oxford: Clarendon Press, 1970).

Haupt, M., 'Varia', *Hermes*, 5 (1871), 21-47.

Heather, Peter, 'Literacy and power in the migration period', in Bowman & Woolf, eds (1994), 177-97.

Hofmann, Michael & Lasdun, James, *After Ovid: New Metamorphoses* (London: Faber & Faber, 1994).

Holden, Anthony, translator, *Greek Pastoral Poetry* (Harmondsworth: Penguin, 1974).

Holst-Warhaft, Gail, *Dangerous Voices: Women's Laments & Greek Literature* (London: Routledge, 1992).

Holum, Kenneth G., *Theodosian Empresses: Women and Imperial Dominion in Late Antiquity* (Berkeley: University of California Press, 1982).

Honig, Edwin, *The Poet's Other Voice: Conversations on Literary Translation* (Amherst: University of Massachusetts Press, 1985).

Irwin, Eleanor, Colour Terms in Greek Poetry (Toronto: Hakkert, 1974).

Jay, Peter, ed., *The Greek Anthology* (Harmondsworth: Penguin, 1973; reprint, 1981).

Johnson, W.R., *The Idea of Lyric* (Berkeley: University of California Press, 1982).

Joyce, James, *Ulysses* (London: Bodley Head, 1936; reprint Harmondsworth: Penguin, 1969).

Kamuf, Peggy, 'Writing Like a Woman', in McConnell-Ginet, Borker & Furman, eds (1980), 284-99.

Kazantzis, Judith, *The Wicked Queen* (London: Sidgwick & Jackson, 1980).

Keeley, Edmund & Sherrard, Philip, translators, *C.P. Cavafy: Collected Poems in English and Greek* (Princeton: Princeton University Press, 1975).

Lefkowitz, Mary, *Heroines and Mysteries* (London: Duckworth, 1981a).

Lefkowitz, Mary, *The Lives of the Greek Poets* (Baltimore & London: Johns Hopkins, 1981b).

Lefkowitz, Mary & Fant, Maureen, *Women's Life in Greece & Rome: A source book in translation* (London: Duckworth, 1982).

Levin, Donald N., 'Quaestiones Erinneanae', *Harvard Studies in Classical Philology*, 66 (1962), 193-204.

Levine, Suzanne Jill, *The Subversive Scribe: Translating Latin American Fiction* (St Paul: Graywolf Press, 1991).

Lisi, Umbertina, *Poetesse Greche* (Catania: Studio Editoriale Moderno, 1933).

Longley, Michael, *The Ghost Orchid* (London: Jonathan Cape, 1995).

Lowe, N.L., 'Sulpicia's Syntax', *Classical Quarterly*, 38 (1988), 193-205.

Luck, George, 'Die Dichterinnen der griechischen Anthologie', *Museum Helveticum*, II (1954), 170-87.

Luck, George, *The Latin Love Elegy* (New York: Barnes & Noble, 1969).

Maier, Carol, 'A Woman in Translation, Reflecting', *Translation Review,* 17 (1985), 4-8.

Maier, Carol, 'Some Thoughts on Translations, Imagination and (Un)academic Activity', *Translation Review*, 26 (1986).

McConnell-Ginet, Sally, Borker, Ruth & Furman, Nelly, *Women and Language in Literature and Society* (New York: Praeger, 1980).

McGrath, Nancy, *Dollarwise Guide to Egypt* (New York: Simon & Schuster, 1982).

McKane, Richard, translator, *Anna Akhmatova: Selected Poems* (Newcastle upon Tyne: Bloodaxe Books, 1989).

Morel, W., *Fragmenta Poetarum Latinorum* (Leipzig, 1927; reprint 1963).

Olsen, Tillie, *Silences* (London: Virago, 1980).

Ostriker, Alicia, 'Body Language: Imagery of the Body in Women's Poetry', in Michaels, Leonard & Ricks, Christopher, eds, *The State of the Language* (Berkeley: University of California Press, 1980), 247-63.

Ostriker, Alicia, 'The Thieves of Language: Women Poets and Revisionist Mythmaking', in Elaine Showalter, ed, *The New Feminist Criticism* (London: Virago, 1986), 314-38.

Page, D.L., *Corinna* (London: Society for the Promotion of Hellenic Studies, 1953).

Parker, Holt, N., 'Other Remarks on the Other Sulpicia', *Classical World*, 86.2 (1992), 89-95.

Parker, Holt, N., 'Sulpicia, The *Auctor de Sulpicia* and the Authorship of 3.9. & 3.11 of the *Corpus Tibullianum*', *Helios*, 21, 1 (1994), 39-62.

Pomeroy, Sarah, *Goddesses, Wives, Whores & Slaves: Women in Classical Antiquity* (New York: Schocken, 1975).

Pomeroy, Sarah, ' "Technikai kai Mousikai": The Education of women in the fourth century and in the Hellenistic Period', *American Journal of Ancient History*, 2 (1977), 51-68.

Pomeroy, Sarah, 'Supplementary Notes on Erinna', *Zeitschrift für Papyrologie und Epigraphik*, 32 (1978), 17-22.

Pomeroy, Sarah, ed., *Woman's History & Ancient History* (Chapel Hill: University of North Carolina Press, 1991).

Pound, Ezra, 'Horace', *The Criterion*, 9 (1929/30); reprinted in *Arion*, 9 (1970), 178-87.

Rabinowitz, N. & Richlin, A., eds, *Feminist Theory & the Classics* (London: Routledge, 1993).

Rayor, Diane, 'Translating Fragments', *Translation Review*, 31-32 (1990), 15-18.

Rayor, Diane, *Sappho's Lyre: Archaic Lyric & Women Poets of Ancient Greece* (Berkeley: University of California Press, 1991).

Rayor, Diane, 'Korinna: Gender & the Narrative Tradition', *Arethusa*, 26 (1993), 219-31.

Rauk, John, 'Erinna's *Distaff* and Sappho Fr.94', *Greek, Roman & Byzantine Studies*, 30 (1989), 99-116.

Rich, Adrienne, *The Fact of a Doorframe: Poems Selected and New 1950-1984* (New York: W.W. Norton, 1984).

Richlin, Amy, 'Sulpicia the Satirist', *Classical World*, 86.2 (1992), 125-39.

St Germain, Sheryl, 'An Interview with Joanna Bankier', *Translation Review*, 17 (1985), 17-20.

Santirocco, M., 'Sulpicia Reconsidered', *Classical Journal*, 74 (1979), 229-38.

Sarton, May, *Collected Poems: 1930-1993* (New York: W.W. Norton, 1994).

Shapcott, Jo, *Phrase Book* (Oxford: Oxford University Press, 1993).

Skinner, Marilyn, 'Briseis, the Trojan Women & Erinna', *Classical World*, 75 (1982), 265-69.

Skinner, Marilyn, 'Corinna of Tanagra and her Audience', *Tulsa Studies in Women's Literature*, 2 (1983), 9-20.

Skinner, Marilyn, 'Greek Women & the Metronymic: A Note on an Epigram by Nossis', *Ancient History Bulletin*, 1 (1987), 39-42.

Skinner, Marilyn, 'Sapphic Nossis', *Arethusa*, 22 (1989), 5-18.

Skinner, Marilyn, 'Nossis Thelyglossos: The Private Text and the Public Book' in Pomeroy, Sarah, ed. (1991), 20-47.

Skinner, Marilyn, 'Women & Language in Archaic Greece, or: Why Is Sappho a Woman?' in Rabinowitz & Richlin, eds (1993), 125-44.

Slings, S.R, *The Poet's 'I' in Archaic Greek Lyric* (Amsterdam: V.U. Press, 1990).

Smith, Kirby Flower, ed. *The Elegies of Albius Tibullus* (1913; reprint, New York: American Books, 1979).

Snyder, McIntosh, J., 'Korinna's "Glorious Songs of Heroes" ', *Eranos*, 82 (1984),123-34.

Snyder, McIntosh, J., *The Woman and the Lyre: Women Writers in Classical Greece and Rome* (Bristol: Bristol Classical Press, 1989).

Snyder, McIntosh, J., 'Public Occasion & Private Passion in the Lyrics of Sappho of Lesbos', in Pomeroy (1991), 1-19.

Stigers, E.S., 'Romantic Sensibility, Poetic Sense: A Response to Hallett on Sappho', *Signs*, 4 (1979), 465-71.

Stigers E.S., 'Sappho's Private World', in Foley (1981), 45-61.

Tannen, Deborah, *Talking from 9 to 5: How Women's and Men's Conversational Styles Affect Who Gets Heard, Who Gets Credit, and What Gets Done* (London: Virago, 1995).

Tarn, W.W., *Hellenistic Civilization* (Cleveland: World Publishing, 1961).

Webster, T.B.L., *Hellenistic Poetry and Art* (New York: Barnes & Noble, 1964).

West, M.L., 'Corinna', *Classical Quarterly*, 20 (1970), 277-87.

West, M.L., 'Erinna', *Zeitschrift für Papyrologie und Epigraphik*, 25 (1977), 95-119.

White, Heather, *Essays in Hellenistic Poetry* (Amsterdam: J.C. Gieben, 1980).

Wilamowitz-Moellendorff, Ulrich von, *Sappho und Simonides* (Berlin: Weidmann, 1913).

Winkler, J.J., 'Gardens of the Nymphs: Public & Private in Sappho's Lyrics', in Foley (1981), 63-89.

Winkler, J.J. *The Constraints of Desire* (London: Routledge, 1990).

Wright. F.A, The Women Poets of Greece, *Fortnightly Review*, n.s. 113 (1923), 322-23.

Yourcenar, Marguerite, *Memoirs of Hadrian*, translated by Grace Frick (London: Secker & Warburg, 1955; reprint, Harmondsworth: Penguin, 1986).